MW00782707

FIELD DRESSING AND BUTCHERING

Rabbits, Squirrels, and Other Small Game

Books by Monte Burch

Field Dressing and Butchering Upland Birds, Waterfowl, and Wild Turkeys
Field Dressing and Butchering Deer
Field Dressing and Butchering Big Game
The Field & Stream All-Terrain-Vehicle Handbook
Denny Brauer's Jig Fishing Secrets
Denny Brauer's Winning Tournament Tactics
Black Bass Basics
Guide to Calling & Rattling Whitetail Bucks
Guide to Successful Turkey Calling
Guide to Calling & Decoying Waterfowl
Guide to Successful Predator Calling
Pocket Guide to Seasonal Largemouth Bass Patterns
Pocket Guide to Seasonal Walleye Tactics
Pocket Guide to Old Time Catfish Techniques
Pocket Guide to Field Dressing, Butchering & Cooking Deer
Pocket Guide to Bowhunting Whitetail Deer
Pocket Guide to Spring & Fall Turkey Hunting
Truman Guide to Fishing, Hunting & Camping
The Pro's Guide to Fishing Missouri Lakes
Waterfowling, A Sportsman's Handbook
Modern Waterfowl Hunting
Shotgunner's Guide
Gun Care and Repair
Outdoorsman's Fix-It Book
Outdoorsman's Workshop
Building and Equipping the Garden and Small Farm Workshop
Basic House Wiring
Complete Guide to Building Log Homes
Children's Toys and Furniture
64 Yard and Garden Projects You Can Build
How to Build 50 Classic Furniture Reproductions
Tile Indoors and Out
The Home Cabinetmaker
How to Build Small Barns & Outbuildings
Masonry & Concrete
Pole Building Projects
Building Small Barns, Sheds & Shelters
Home Canning & Preserving (w/Joan Burch)
Building Mediterranean Furniture (w/Jay Hedden)
Fireplaces (w/Robert Jones)
The Homeowner's Complete Manual of Repair and Improvement (w/3 others)
The Good Earth Almanac Series
Survival Handbook
Old-Time Recipes
Natural Gardening Handbook

FIELD DRESSING AND BUTCHERING
Rabbits, Squirrels, and Other Small Game

Step-by-Step Instructions, from Field to Table

Monte Burch

The Lyons Press
Guilford, Connecticut
An imprint of The Globe Pequot Press

The Lyons Press is an imprint of The Globe Pequot Press.

Printed in the United States of America

Designed by Compset, Inc.

10 9 8 7 6 5 4 3

Library of Congress Cataloging-in-Publication Data is available on
file.

Contents

Introduction

A variety of small game species has provided food, fur, and other valuable commodities to humans almost from our beginnings as a species. In North America small game was a valued part of the Native American's life; game such as the beaver was often called "little brother." Small game was also a valued food source for the early European settlers, and of course a great deal of the continent was explored in the search for small game pelts. By the turn of the 20th century small game was a staple food in many of the bigger city restaurants, with barrels of salted food shipped regularly to market.

My father used to tell me about the youngsters in his community hunting jackrabbits for market. They hunted as a group. Most of the jackrabbits were gone when I was growing up. This was not due entirely to market hunting; the main reason was the changing of the countryside from prairie to small grain fields. Cottontails were on the rise, however (along with numerous other small game species), and the local farm co-op paid good money for rabbits as well as small game pelts.

In my youth I quickly discovered trapping. Trapping paid good money to a grade-schooler during the early 1950s, but mostly I enjoyed the excuse for being outdoors. Back in those days there were no wild turkeys or deer in my part of the country. Small game, however, abounded due to the patchwork of small fields, overgrown hedgerows, and woodlots. Small game was a regular repast for our family, as it was for most of the other families in our community. Squirrels, rabbits, raccoons, and opossums all made it to the dinner table. Rabbit skins were tanned and used for glove linings.

An interesting aside: My dad's uncle once handmade a banjo for him when he was a youngster. He bent the head from green wood, using a cut-down ivory comb for the bridge; most interesting, the head was covered with a groundhog skin, cured green into

Small game have provided food, fur, and other valuable commodities almost from the dawn of humankind.

rawhide. The banjo, a valued family heirloom, still has excellent sound.

Small game species abound in many parts of the country, at least where land is not covered by the ever-increasing concrete sprawl or suburban and rural land development. Some developed areas are seeing growing populations of species that have learned to live off or with mankind. Raccoons, groundhogs, squirrels, and opossums have become quite "urbanized."

Small game includes such critters as rabbits, squirrels, and groundhogs, as well as furbearers such as opossums, raccoons, muskrats, and beavers. The methods of dressing and cooking differ with the various species, the age of the animal, and whether or not the fur is to be kept. Along with directions for skinning and dressing each type of small game, I have also included general cooking information as well as numerous recipes.

CHAPTER

1

Tools and Equipment

The first item you'll need is a good sharp knife. You can skin and cut up small game with nothing more than a sharp pocketknife—in fact, many traditional knife companies produce pocket skinning knives for just this purpose. Small skinning knives featuring gut hooks can also be used for quick and easy skinning. Special skinning knives are also available from trapping supply houses. For butchering and cutting up game at home, regular butcher knives are a good choice.

Knives are available in a variety of steels, ranging from stainless through several grades of carbon steel and combinations of steel. Stainless-steel knives are the hardest; soft carbon steel the softest. Stainless steel requires a great deal more effort to sharpen, but it holds an edge longer than carbon metals. I prefer a stainless-steel knife for field dressing but use carbon-steel knives for butchering. I don't have to worry about a stainless-steel field-dressing knife quickly becoming dull while on a hunt; nor does it rust from bloodstains if not immediately cleaned and dried properly. Carbon butcher knives, on the other hand, offer quicker touch-up with a butcher's steel or hone during the butchering process.

A good pair of heavy-duty game shears can also be invaluable. The Chef'sChoice models are made of stainless steel and feature a take-down design that allows for easy cleanup, even in the dishwasher.

Regardless of what type of knife and metal you use, it's extremely important to have the knife as sharp as possible when you're field dressing, skinning or cutting up small game. In fact, when skinning and cutting up game at home, I keep several knives sharpened and ready to use so I don't have to stop and sharpen or hone a blade during the process.

1

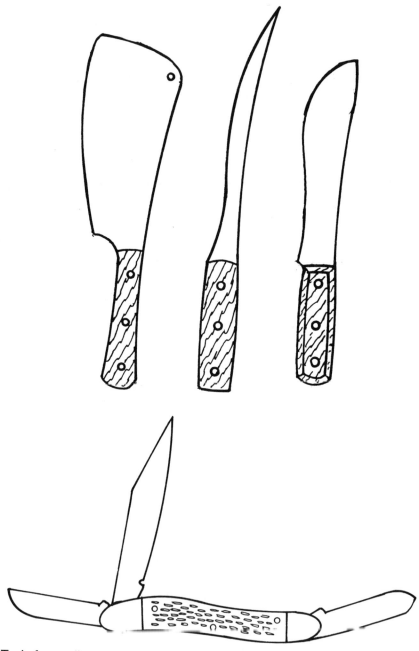

Tools for small game range from a simple pocketknife to a variety of skinning and butchering knives.

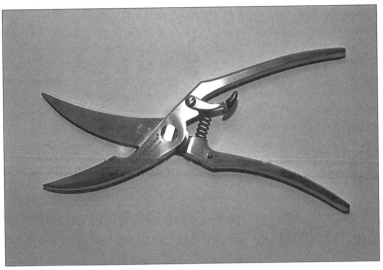

A pair of cleanable, high-quality game shears can also be a great help.

A wide variety of sharpening devices is available, ranging from simple handheld stones to electric grinding wheels. My grandfather's old foot-turned grinding wheel did a great job of sharpening knives, and many of today's electric wheels offer the same quality of sharpening. Again, one of my favorites is the Chef'sChoice

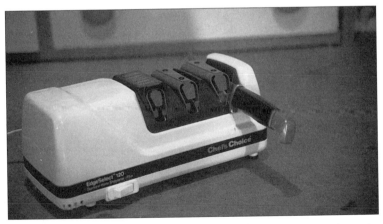

Regardless of the knife you use, it's extremely important to keep it sharp. Any number of sharpening devices is available, ranging from simple hones to electric-powered models.

model. A small sharpening hone or device kept in your pocket or hunting pack can also be used to keep an edge on a blade.

Although some small game species, such as squirrels and rabbits, are easily skinned in the field, others are best skinned back at home or camp. A gambrel on which to hang the critter makes the

When cleaning and dressing small game, it's a good idea to wear plastic gloves to prevent the possibilities of transmitting tickborne diseases.

chore much easier. Gambrels are available from trapping supply houses in a variety of sizes. You can also make up your own gambrel quite easily. The homemade model shown on page 44 can be used for deer and small game. Small game is hung by using the adjustable hooks in the holes in the bottom bar. If you intend to keep or sell the fur, you'll need other fur-working tools, including a fleshing knife, a fleshing beam, and stretching frames.

You should always wear disposable protective gloves when field dressing, skinning, or dressing any small game. This is primarily due to the fact that the fur of small game animals can harbor ticks and disease pathogens. Make sure you clean all utensils used for dressing small game in hot soapy water. Adding a small amount of laundry bleach to the water helps disinfect the tools. Rinse well.

It's also important to think about the cutting surfaces you use when cutting up meat. Although wooden cutting boards are traditional, they are more difficult to clean and sanitize than some of the newer surfaces. Once wooden cutting boards become deeply grooved from knives, it becomes especially hard to completely remove blood and meat particles from them. The best cutting surfaces don't become grooved with knife cuts and can be easily cleaned

Cutting boards are extremely important. Synthetic boards are more easily cleaned than wooden—most go directly into automatic dishwashers.

and sanitized. Also, make sure that the surface you choose doesn't dull your knife blade too quickly. It's a good idea to have one large surface, or at least a couple of smaller ones. My dad ran a cabinet shop for years, and we recycled plastic laminate sink cutouts as cutting boards. These work well, but they still became damaged over time and should be replaced.

WORK SPACE

You can, of course, skin, dress, and prepare small game on your kitchen table or counter, but you probably don't want to. It's a

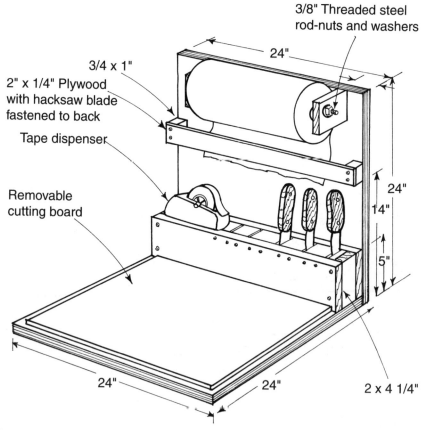

A place to work is important. A table set up in a shop, garage, or even outside is best. An organizer for your butcher table can also help.

messy chore at best, and some small game animals emit a distinct odor during the skinning and butchering process. It's best to use a space set aside for the chore, outdoors or in a garage or outbuilding. This space doesn't have to be elaborate or involve a lot of square footage. And you can use it for other projects when it's not needed for game cleaning.

You'll need a sturdy table with an easily cleanable top. This can be a plastic laminate; if your tabletop is wood, you can simply use an oilcloth or disposable plastic tablecloth for butchering. One of the best surfaces is stainless steel. It hoses down and cleans up easily and is sturdy and hard surfaced. You'll still need a separate cutting surface atop the stainless steel, because stainless will scratch, and it also quickly dulls knife blades. Several years ago I bought two used stainless-steel school cafeteria kitchen tables at an auction, and they've turned out to be one of my best investments. I have one set up outside next to my garage with a work light over it and an outside plug and hose nearby. I use this area for everything from filleting fish to dressing wild turkeys and waterfowl, skinning small game, and cutting up deer. I have the other table in my garage for weather protection and for those days when it's too hot or too cold to butcher outdoors. Both tables were fairly low, so I added leg extenders to raise them to a comfortable, 36-inch-high working height. Low tables can cause back problems if you spend long hours standing slightly bent while grinding or cutting up meat. Several years ago I constructed a table just for butchering, making it the correct height and covered with plastic laminate for easy cleanup.

You'll find sources of butchering supplies, including cutting boards and tables, listed in the back of this book.

OTHER TOOLS

All game animals should be kept cool from the moment they're taken, and that means keeping them in a cooler with ice on hot days, or making sure they're hung in an area with plenty of ventilation. I've also used an old refrigerator to hold field-dressed game for a couple of days before I finally butchered it. I think this has some of the same benefits as hanging big game in cool lockers.

Other items you'll need include pans to hold the meat as you butcher. Large plastic tubs can be used to hold meat cuts to be

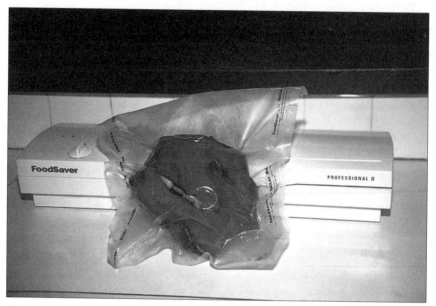

A vacuum bagger is an excellent tool for preparing meat for freezing.

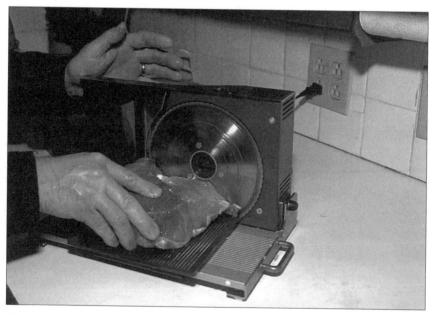

An electric food slicer can make short work of slicing chores. The new folding Chef'sChoice slicer from EdgeCraft makes packing a slicer for hunting camp easy. It's also easy to store at home.

ground. Lots of clean, soft rags are also important for wiping and cleaning your hands, cleaning surfaces, and removing hair from knife blades and hands. Another excellent tool is a vacuum bagger, such as the FoodSaver, for preparing game for freezing. If you can your small game, you'll need a pressure canner, jars, and other equipment. An electric grinder for making game sausage, an electric food slicer for slicing meat, and a dehydrator for jerky can also make food preparation chores easier.

CHAPTER 2

Rabbits

It was the day after Christmas and it was obvious that 12-year-old
Mark was enjoying his Christmas presents. He was sporting a
new pair of insulated overalls and his very own game vest. He
was also carrying his mom's borrowed shotgun, which suited his
small frame.

"Whoa, hold it a minute," I told the eager youngster as his fast
pace carried him by another brushpile. "You've got to take it slow
when kicking up rabbits." He went to the pile, gave it a hearty
kick—and nothing! He looked at me with a shrug. That's when I
saw the form dart from beneath his feet and spring through the foot
of powder snow toward another brushpile farther down the
hedgerow. The little 20-gauge came up fast and snow flew in a puff
behind the bounding bunny, but he made the safety of the pile with
time to spare. I saw the rabbit duck through the brushpile, pause
another moment, then slip on ahead of us down the hedgerow.

I could tell as Mark removed his spent shell that he was disap-
pointed. I figured it was a good lesson and would slow his energetic
walk down to something more like hunting. He didn't miss the next
dozen or so brushpiles, but he still had no luck. Then I saw a form
hunkered below an overhanging snow cornice over a wild rosebush.

"Mark," I softly called, "over here." We both worked our way
cautiously toward the still form. With an explosion of snow, the cot-
tontail leaped from the rosebush. This time Mark lucked out, rolling
the rabbit within 25 feet or so from the end of his muzzle. He hefted
the fat bunny, grinned, and admired the soft fur. Then we stuffed the
rabbit in the back of his new game vest.

An hour later Mark's energy was fading: With the heavy rubber
boots, the new but heavy and stiff overalls, and about 10 pounds of
rabbit in the back of his vest (which I might add was loaded with

Rabbits continue to be one of America's most popular game animals, supplying lots of hunters with fun, excitement, and great meat for the table.

shells in every pocket and corner), he could barely slog his feet through the drifts of snow. He was a tired little boy, but still bubbling with excitement to tell Mom about his experiences as we made our way back toward the house in the fast-approaching evening gloom.

Cottontails and snow—that's the epitome of rabbit hunting to me. To some folks, it's running bunnies with a pack of beagles, and that too can provide great fun and excitement. For other hunters its swamp rabbits, snowshoes, or varying hares. And in the Southwest, it's jackrabbits.

Regardless of how they're taken, rabbits have been important small game for millennia. They're still some of the most popular hunted animals, especially cottontails.

FIELD DRESSING RABBITS

As with any game, rabbits should be properly taken care of in the field to assure good-quality meat. They should be field dressed as soon as possible. Some hunters like to gut rabbits as soon as they're shot. If the weather is cold—as it often is when you're rabbit hunting—some hunters prefer to field dress and skin the rabbits all in one operation, at the end of the hunt.

Eviscerating or gutting in the field is quite easy. Make a cut with a sharp knife from the tail to the throat, through the pelvic bone to

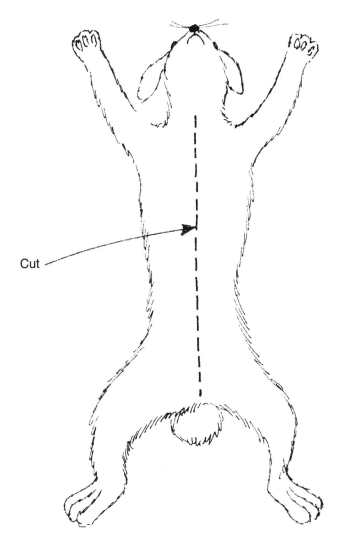

Cut

If the weather is warm, or you plan to be in the field for some time, field dressing is important. Make a cut from the vent to the throat with a sharp knife. The entrails can then be "flipped" out or pulled out by hand. You should wear gloves while doing this.

separate the hips, and through the ribs up to the throat. Then grasp the rabbit by the hind legs and whirl it around your head like a slingshot. The entrails will pull out and be thrown clear. When my dad and other youngsters in his neighborhood hunted rabbits for the market many, many years ago and it came time for them to gut a hundred or so bunnies, gut-flinging at buddies was not unusual. You can also simply pull out the entrails with your hand.

Skinning Rabbits

A more modern and less messy method is to first skin the animal and then eviscerate. Skinning rabbits is easy, because the skin comes off like a glove. One method, if you don't intend to use the fur, is to make a small cut in the skin at the top of the back using a sharp knife. Grasp each half of the skin and pull outward to peel it off both ends of the rabbit. It will pull off extremely easily, especially if the carcass is warm. Then cut off the head and feet with the skin attached to them.

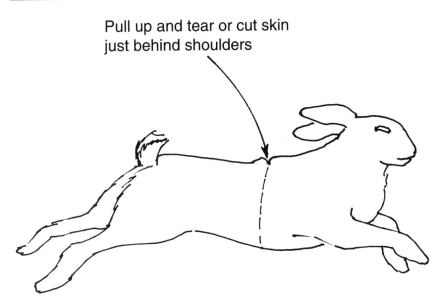

Pull up and tear or cut skin
just behind shoulders

In many instances, especially if the weather is cold, you may want to wait until the hunt is over, then skin and eviscerate all the animals at once. In this case the first step is to make a cut just through the skin at the top of the back. Wear protective gloves while doing this.

Grasp the skin on each side of the cut and pull sideways. Rabbit skin will peel off quite easily.

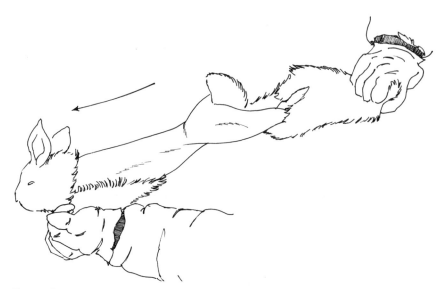

Grasp the hind feet and continue peeling the front portion of the skin down over the front legs to the front feet and to the head. Turn the rabbit and peel the front portion of the skin down over the hind legs.

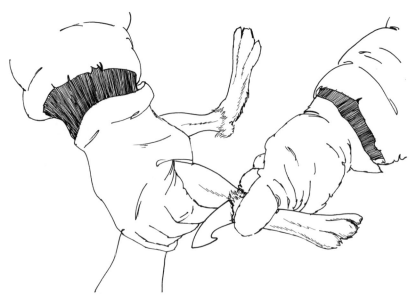

Bend and cut off the back feet at the joint. Cut off the head and front feet.

Slit the carcass down the middle, starting at the top of the rib cage and continuing down to the vent.

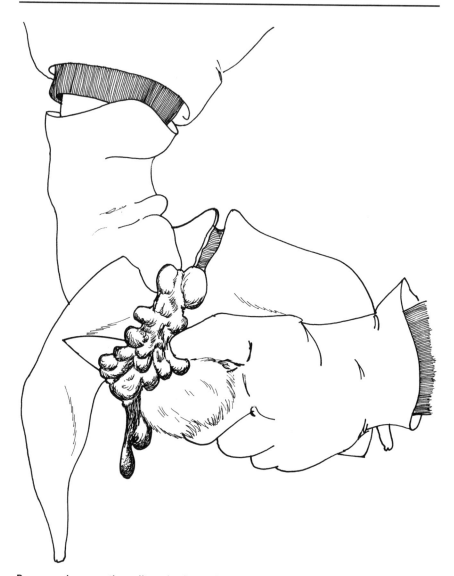

Remove the entrails, pulling the lungs, heart, and windpipe downward and out of the chest cavity. Cut off the tail and vent area with entrails attached.

If you wish to keep the skin, skin in the open-case method. Make a cut along the belly from the tail to the underside of the chin, taking care not to cut through the belly muscle. Then make a cut along the bottom side of each leg to the belly cut. Gently pull the

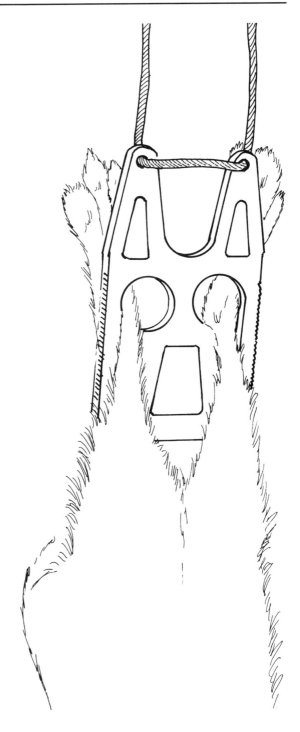

If you prefer to keep the skin intact, hang the rabbit in a rabbit/squirrel gambrel, then slit the belly and inside the legs. Cut around the feet and peel off the skin.

skin away. Rabbit skin is very thin and tears quite easily, but it makes a great glove liner when tanned.

To eviscerate, make a slit in the skin and muscle, but not into the entrails, from just in front of the vent up to the throat. Cut through the rib cage as you make this cut. Cut through the pelvic

Several small gambrels are available for skinning rabbits and squirrels.

bone, being careful not to cut into the genitals, entrails, or anus. Pop open the pelvic bone and use the knife to cut around and en- circle the anus. Reach inside the opened rib cage, grasp the lungs and heart, and pull down. This will remove those organs as well as the entrails. As the entrails are gently pulled through the pelvic arch, they will take the genitals and anus with them, all in one piece. Wash the carcass in cold water.

TULAREMIA

One problem with rabbits is that they sometimes carry "rabbit fever" or tularemia. This bacterial disease can be transmitted to humans and should not be taken lightly. However, it isn't a reason to avoid hunting rabbits either. Understanding the disease and how it's trans- mitted can put unfounded fears to rest.

Tularemia is recorded in more than 80 species of mammals, in- cluding rabbits. However, it's not as common in cottontails as is sometimes believed. In a Missouri study that analyzed more than 12,000 dead rabbits, only 2 were found infected with tularemia. A Kansas study indicate that 16 percent of rabbits found dead within a study area carried the disease.

Ticks, flies, lice, and fleas transmit the disease among animals, and the old advice to "wait until the first hard freeze" before hunt- ing rabbits is based on the assumption that when these insect vec- tors are killed by cold weather, there is no longer reason to worry. Humans can contract tularemia by drinking contaminated water, being bitten by an infected tick or other insect, or handling diseased animals. Rabbits, the most common animal vector, account for 13 percent of the known tularemia cases in humans.

Although only a small segment of the rabbit population may be affected by the disease, it's wise to consider the potential danger. Tularemia is always fatal to rabbits, usually within seven days of in- fection. The rabbit immediately becomes sluggish, sick, and clumsy. For this reason, simply avoid shooting an animal that isn't wary, stumbles while running, or is easily caught by beagles.

Tularemia bacteria are present on a rabbit's fur and in its inter- nal organs and body fluids. The bacteria are destroyed by cooking, so the only way you can be exposed is through handling the car- cass. The bacteria don't enter healthy skin, but infect a human through cuts or scratches. Rubber gloves or disposable plastic gloves allow you to handle infected animals safely.

When a rabbit is cleaned, the liver may provide evidence of an early infection. A healthy rabbit liver is a dark reddish purple, with neither discolorations nor spotting. Many rabbits carry bladder-worms, which cause large white spots of scar tissue on the liver but do not affect the edibility of the meat. However, when tularemia is present, the liver swells and is speckled with tiny white dots. These are likened to stars in the sky on a very clear night.

If you suspect that you've contacted an infected animal, be alert for chills, fever, and swollen lymph glands within several days. Report to your doctor immediately.

CHAPTER 3

Squirrels

Even though dawn was just breaking, the mulberry was already alive with squirrels when I eased beneath a nearby tree and sat down. I counted nine bushytails—I think. It was hard to tell with all the commotion in the berry-laden tree. I waited until one of the scurrying creatures provided a clear shot, raised my old Remington .22, and eased back the trigger. A sharp crack broke the

Squirrels provide some of the best traditional hunting. Squirrel hunting runs from summer through fall and even into winter. Squirrels are also a favored game food.

summer morning stillness and the fox squirrel hesitated for a moment, then dropped to the ground with a thump. I noted the exact location and remained still. All movement halted for no more than a minute. Then I spotted a branch shaking and the action started all over again. In less than half an hour I had collected a half-dozen squirrels—four fox and two gray—and filled a plastic bag with mulberries for a pie. Fried young squirrel and mulberry pie—a great morning.

Whether you're hunting summer squirrels on mulberries or autumn squirrels when they begin working the nut trees, it's fun, relaxing, and a great way to sharpen woodsman skills. Squirrel hunting is also a fine way to introduce youngsters or newcomers to hunting. And of course the end result is a tasty dinner.

DRESSING SQUIRRELS

The problem, however, is that squirrels—especially older ones—are tough to skin and dress. Squirrels can be dressed with several methods: by hanging them in a game holder, in much the same manner as for other furbearers; by splitting the skin across the back, in the same manner illustrated for rabbits; with the open-pelt fur skinning method; or with a totally different method—an old American Indian method.

To dress with a game holder, suspend the holder from a tree or a post at about shoulder height. Holding the squirrel belly-out and head-down, push its back legs firmly into the holder's outer holding Vs of the holder. Cut through the root of the tail, leaving the skin on top intact. Then use a blunt-tipped small blade to make diagonal cuts to the belly on both sides. Pull the hide down over the head, remove the front feet, and skin out the head; or you can cut the hide off just past the nose. You can also skin down to the head and leave the hide attached if you won't be eating that old-time delicacy—squirrel brains.

Then reverse the squirrel, placing its neck in the center V of the game holder, and skin the belly and hindquarters. Cut off the back feet. Use a blunt-tipped blade to eviscerate the animal from the neck down through and out the pelvic arch without puncturing the intestines or bladder.

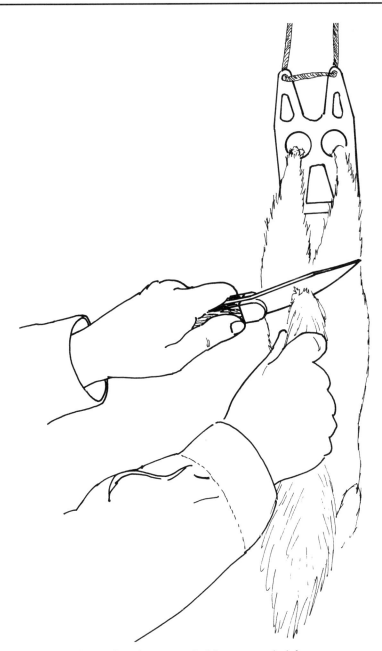

Squirrels can be dressed with a game holder suspended from a tree or post. Push the back legs firmly into the Vs of the holder. Cut through the root of the tail, leaving the skin on the back intact.

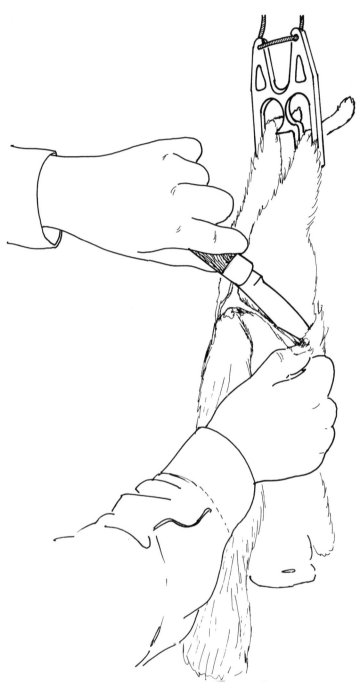

Then make diagonal cuts from the root of the tail to the belly on both sides.

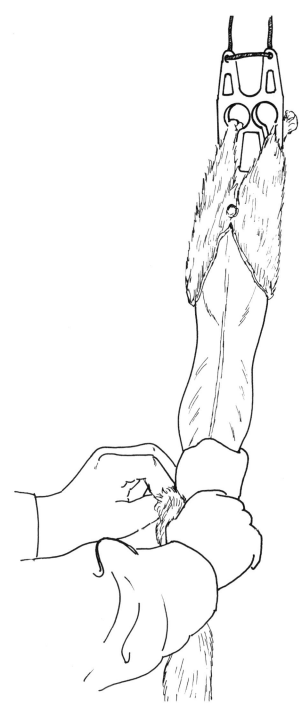

Pull the skin off the
back, front legs, and
head by pulling down-
ward on the tail. Skin
out the head if you
want to keep it for
squirrel brains or
other delicacies.

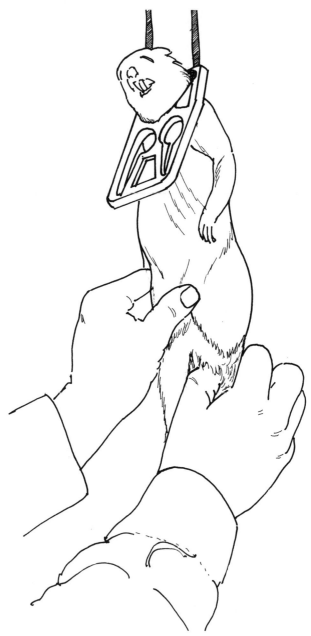

Even if you don't want to keep the head, leave it on the skin at this time. Turn the squirrel upright and hang by its head in the skinning gambrel. Grasp the skin on the point of the belly and pull down to remove the skin from the back legs.

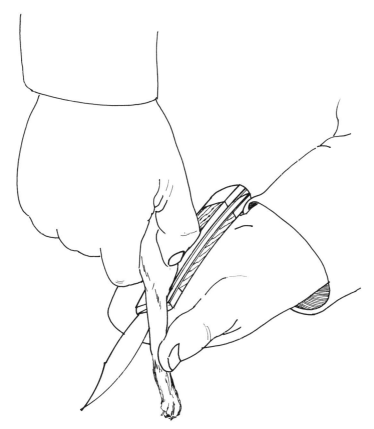

The squirrel can also be eviscerated while hanging in the gambrel.
Then cut off the head and feet.

SKINNING SQUIRRELS

Squirrels can also be skinned in the same manner as for rabbits. Make a 2-inch cut through the skin across the back and about halfway between the head and tail. Insert the fingers of each hand under the skin and pull in opposite directions. This peels the fore-part forward and the rear part to the tail, peeling off the skin. This isn't easy to do—it takes quite a bit of effort—but the skin won't tear (as it will with rabbits). Cut off the feet, head, and tail as the skin reaches those areas.

Squirrels can be dressed in another method I learned from my Ozark uncle a long time ago. He told me that he'd learned it from some of our American Indian relatives. Once you learn the technique, it's quick and easy. With a little practice you can dress a squirrel in a couple of minutes. Having water nearby can make the chore easier, but it's not necessary. You can cut off the front feet, but leave the rear feet in place, or leave all four feet in place.

Position the squirrel on its belly and, holding the tail with one hand, place your foot on a rear leg and make a cut across the underside of the tail at its base and completely through the tailbone, but leaving the top of the tail skin attached. Continue the cut about an inch or so up the hip of each hind leg. This cut is somewhat difficult, but easier if you pinch and pull up the skin then slide the knife underneath, cutting with the blade outward, instead of attempting to saw through the skin.

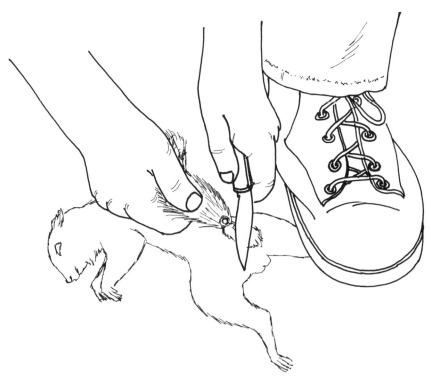

Another method can also be used to skin squirrels. Make a cut through the underside of the tail at the root, leaving the top of the tail skin attached.

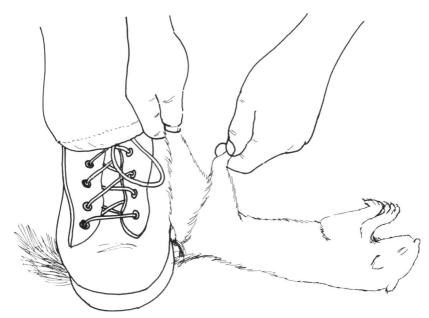

With the squirrel on a solid, flat surface, stand on its tail and grasp the hind legs.

Place the squirrel on a solid surface and position your foot on the underside of its tail. Pull upward on the hind legs. The skin in front of the hind legs will peel off up to the head and over the front legs. Then place your foot on the peeled-down skin section, use a knife to gently loosen the skin on the belly, and peel it back off the hips and up to the hind feet. Continue peeling the skin over the legs to the feet, cutting them off at the first joint.

If you don't want the head, cut it off along with the front skin section. If you'd prefer to maintain the head on the carcass, work the skin off the head with short, light strokes and remove the eyes.

To eviscerate, use a sharp knife to make a cut through the squirrel's chest wall, through its ribs, and down its belly through the pelvic girdle that lies over the rectal area. Be careful not to puncture the entrails. The entrails can then easily be pulled from the body cavity, and removed along with the anus and genitals.

Pulling up on the hind legs will peel the skin away from the majority of the squir-rel's front portion.

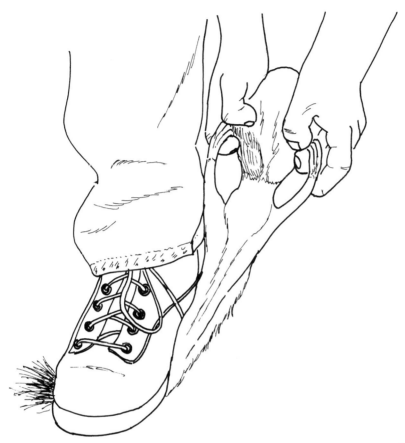

Grasp the squirrel between the head and the front legs and continue peeling until the skin reaches the front feet and head.

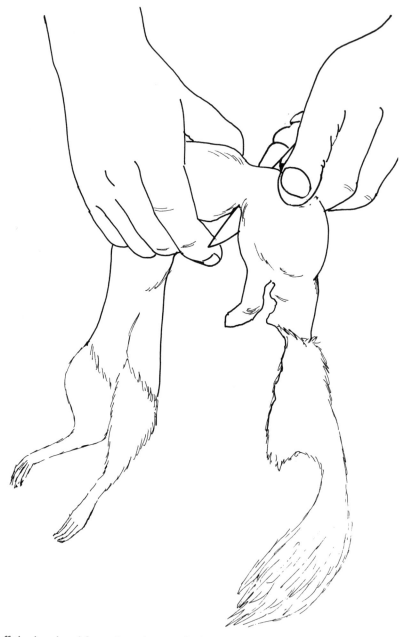

Cut off the head and front feet along with the majority of the skin.

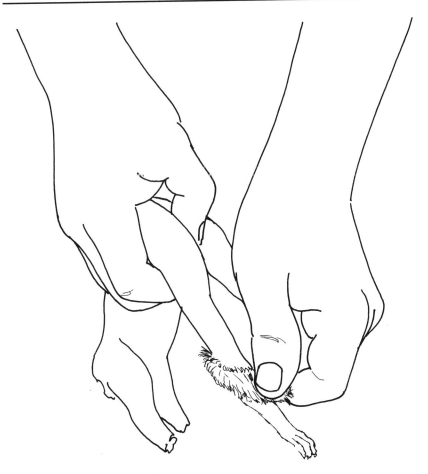

Peel the skin off the rear legs.

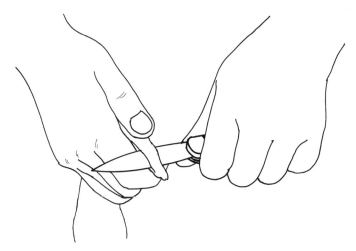

Then cut off the rear legs.

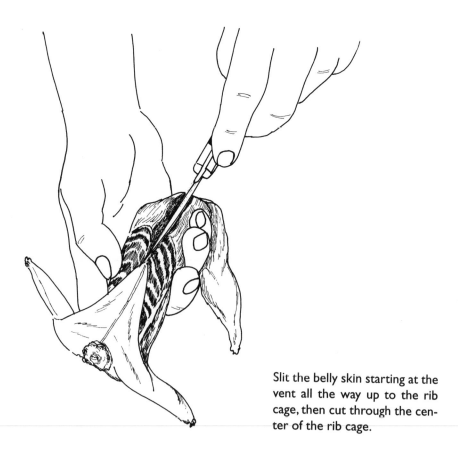

Slit the belly skin starting at the vent all the way up to the rib cage, then cut through the center of the rib cage.

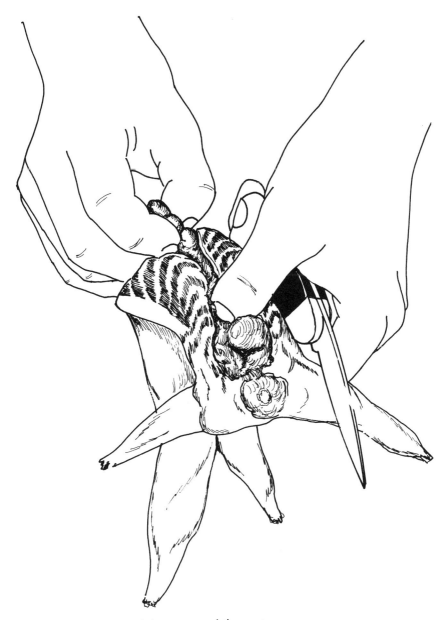

Pull the entrails out and down toward the vent.

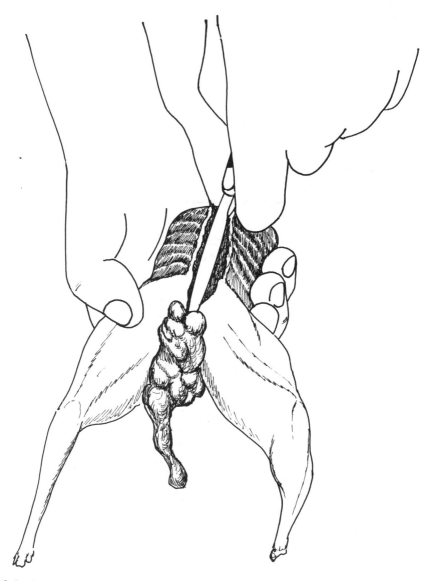

Split the pelvic bone, cut around the vent, and remove the entrails and vent all in one.

AGING SQUIRRELS

It's important to determine if a squirrel is young or old. Older squirrels can be tougher than the proverbial boot if not cooked properly, while young squirrels can be prepared in any number of ways. Small squirrels that skin easily are usually the young of the year. The scrotum on older male squirrels tends to be large, blackened, and wrinkled with little hair, while the scrotum on younger males is smaller, smooth, and usually covered with hair. The nipples on older females tend to be prominent and dark; those on younger squirrels are smaller and lighter in color.

CLEANING AND CUTTING UP SQUIRRELS

No matter how you clean and cut up a squirrel, you're going to get some hair on the carcass, and it can be the very devil to remove. Washing the carcass immediately after skinning in cold running water can alleviate some of the problem, but you'll probably have to pick off some hair even after washing. Make sure you trim away any shot-damaged meat. Soaking the meat overnight in a cold salt water or a vinegar/water solution can improve its flavor, especially on older animals.

After they're skinned and eviscerated, squirrels and rabbits are normally quartered. Pressing down or twisting down on the rear

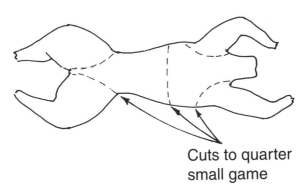

Cuts to quarter
small game

Squirrels and rabbits are normally quartered; you can also leave small animals whole for freezing.

legs dislocates the hip joint; the rear leg is then cut away from the carcass at the dislocated joint. Repeat for the opposite leg. The front shoulder is removed by sliding a knife down between the shoulder girdle and the rib cage. These pieces can be used for frying, if it's a young animal. This leaves the back, rib cage, and neck. The larger meat on each side of the back can be boned out and fried as well. Or you can cut away the back, rib cage, and neck meat, dice it up, and use it for soup stock or stews. With older animals the entire carcass is used for stews, but it can still be quartered in the same manner. You can also place a whole squirrel or rabbit in a pressure cooker, then remove the meat from the bones when it's cooked. Grind the meat for sandwiches, or dice it and use it in casseroles.

Furred Small Game

F urred small game includes beavers, muskrats, raccoons, opossums, and groundhogs. Not only are these critters excellent on the table, but they also provide fur, once a valuable commodity. Many of these small game animals are taken by hunting, with "coon hunting" with dogs a nighttime tradition of the South and Midwest. Groundhogs or woodchucks are often hunted as varmints with long-range rifles—an excellent sport and one that almost any farmer will appreciate, because groundhog den holes can create a number of problems. Muskrats and beavers are more commonly

Small furred game such as opossums, raccoons, groundhogs, muskrats, and beavers have traditionally provided food for the table.

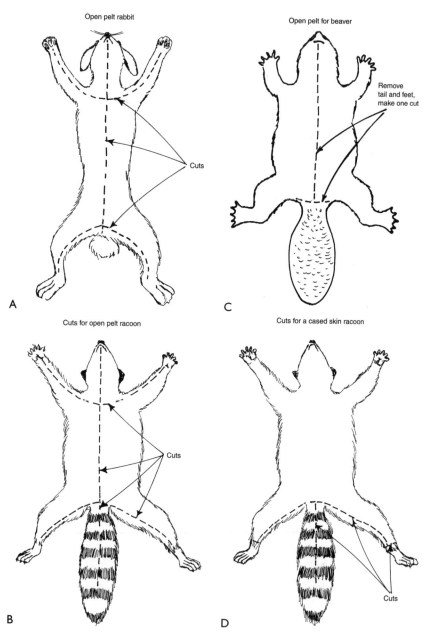

Small furred game can be skinned in one of two methods, open or cased skin.
A. Open-pelt rabbit.
B. Open-pelt raccoon.
C. Open-pelt beaver.
D. Cased-skin raccoon.

trapped, although nuisance animals are sometimes hunted. Understanding the habits of each animal is important not only when you're hunting or trapping them, but also for determining their edibility and how they should be prepared and cooked.

SKINNING

Furbearing game can be skinned in one of two methods: open skin and cased skin. An open skin is actually the skin opened up and stretched out. Open-skin dressed furs can be used as wall hangings

In most instances it's easiest to skin small game while suspended in a gambrel. A number of gambrels are available commercially.

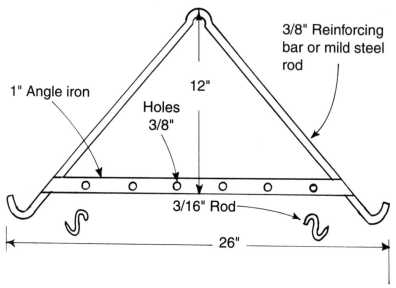

Or you can make up your own. The gambrel shown can be used for deer or small game.

or rugs. In the cased-skin method the skin is peeled off, like pulling off a sock wrong-side out. These skins are then dried over a fur stretcher. Although the animal can be skinned by laying the carcass belly-side-up on a table, it's easiest to skin using a gambrel, or even by tying up one rear leg and hanging the animal head-down.

Cased Skin

Cased skin is the method most often used when the fur of raccoons, opossums, and muskrats is to be sold. Insert a knife point at the heel of the rear foot and slit the skin to just about an inch forward of the anus. Repeat on the opposite leg, then join the two cuts together. These cuts are best made with the legs well stretched out and the skin fairly tight. For this reason, a gambrel makes the chore easier. Do not cut into the muscle, but hold the knife blade-outward to make the cuts.

At this point, make a cut encircling the ankle of each leg at the beginning of the heel cut. Work the skin off the leg, starting with the loose flap that you created by making the encircling cut. On tougher-skinned animals such as raccoons, a piece of steel rod with

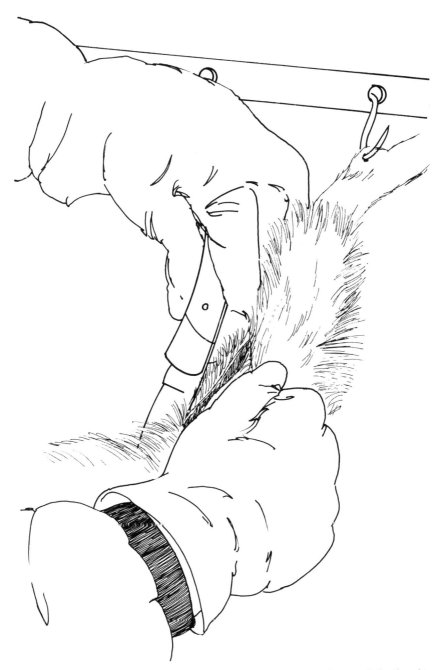

For a cased skin, insert a knife point at the heel of the rear foot and slit the skin to the anus. Then repeat the step from the opposite foot to complete the cut.

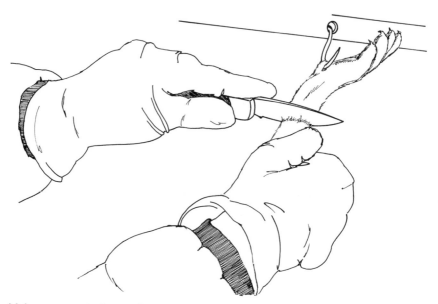

Make a cut encircling each ankle at the beginning cut.

Work the skin off one leg, using a knife to help cut it away.

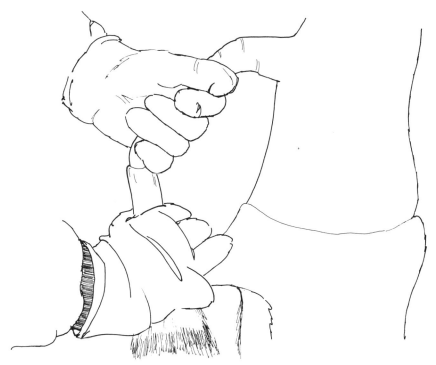

You can either slit the tail or peel it off.

the skin wrapped around it provides a good grip for pulling the skin downward. As you pull the skin downward, work your fingers between the skin and muscle to release the skin.

On muskrats, beavers, and opossums, the tail is not skinned out but removed before skinning. Raccoon tails are usually left on the hide. If you're going to skin the tail, make a short cut up on the tail's underside, working your fingers around to peel the skin away from the sides and the back of the tail. A trapper's tail stripper (a clamp-on-type plier) slides over the tailbone to help apply pressure as you remove the tail skin. Work your fingers around the tail to pull the skin away from the tail and then down along the back of the animal. A partially split stick can also be used as a tail stripper.

The skin is then peeled down off the rest of the body to the head and front legs. Use a knife only when necessary. Peel the skin down over the front legs and then cut them off above the front foot.

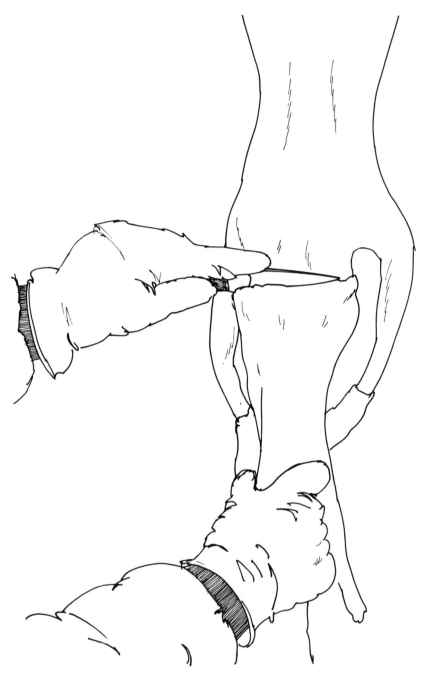

Use the knife to cut away the hide, and work your fingers between the skin and muscle to continue peeling off the hide.

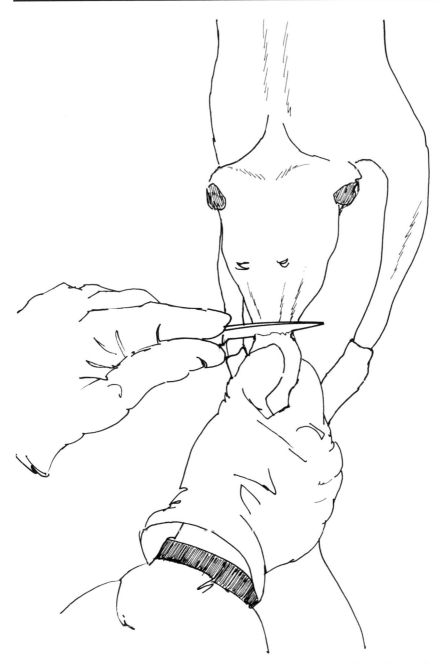

Skin out the head, taking extra care not to cut through the skin and ruin the pelt. Cut off the skin at the tip of the nose, leaving the nose tip on the pelt. Cut off the feet.

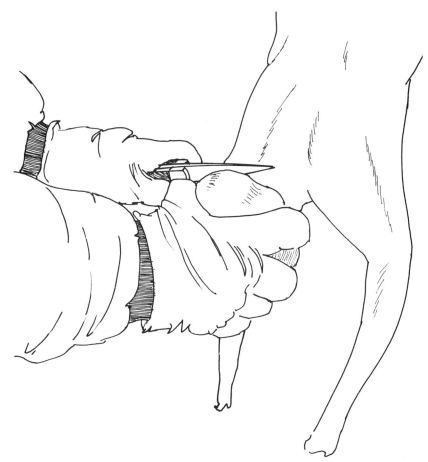

Cut off the head.

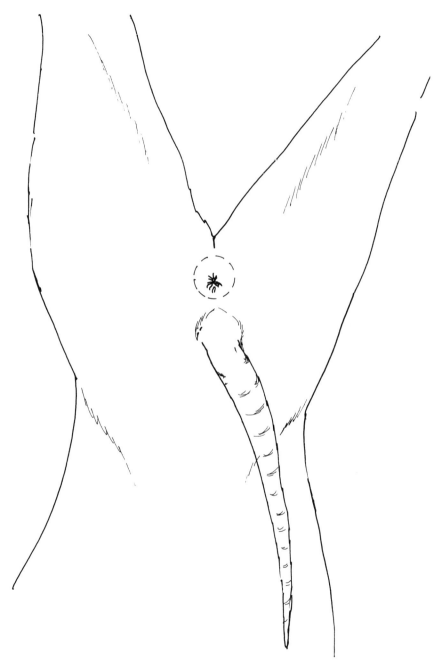

Use a sharp-pointed knife to encircle the anus.

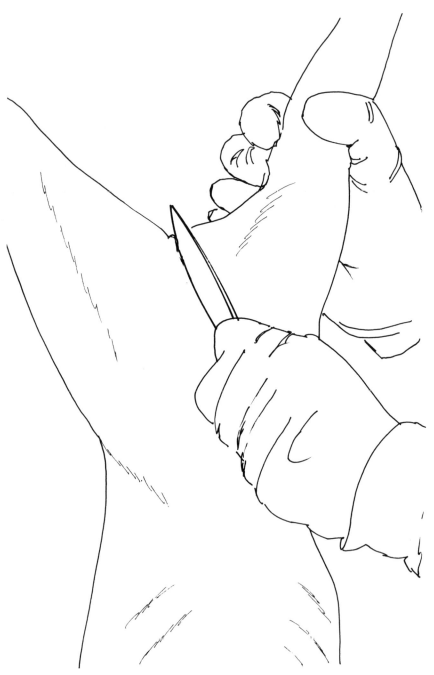

Cut through the pelvic bone.

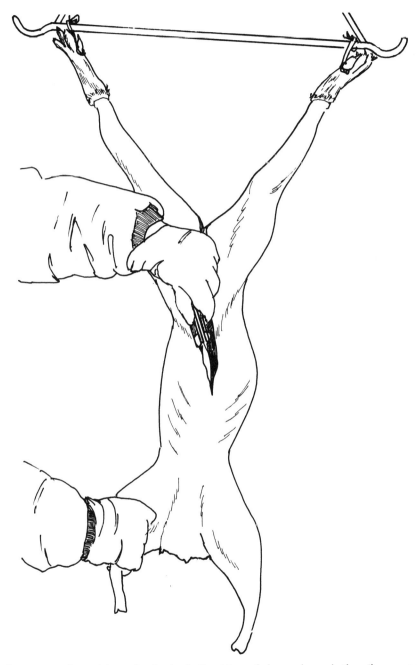

Starting at the pelvic arch, slit the belly skin and down through the rib cage to the neck.

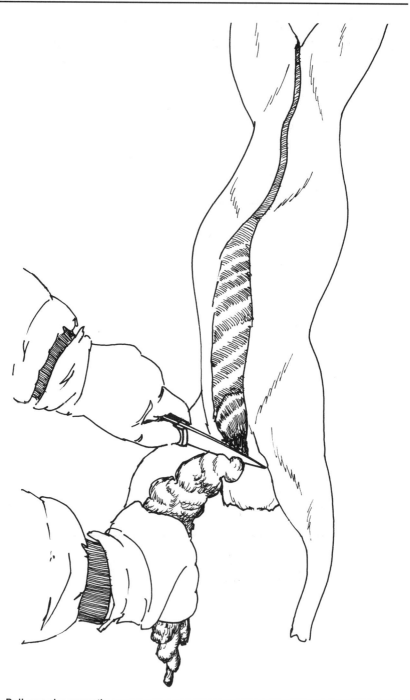

Pull out the entrails.

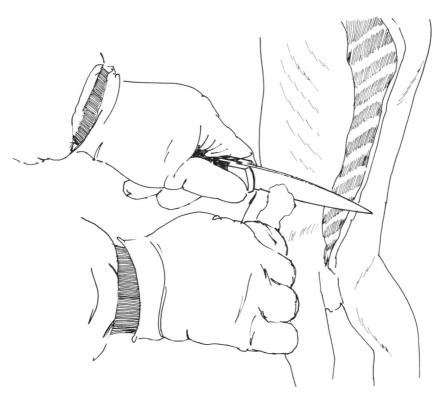

Remove the scent glands.

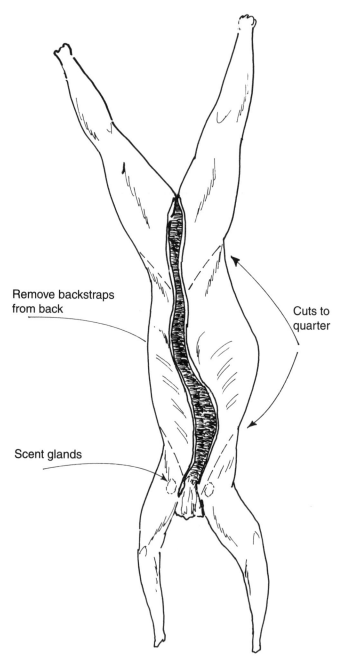

Remove backstraps
from back

Cuts to
quarter

Scent glands

Small game can be quartered or cut into chunks.

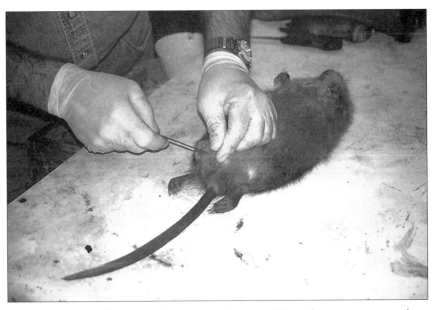

Muskrats are usually skinned in the cased method. Your first step is to make a slit from the inside of a rear heel to the opposite heel.

Cut off the tail.

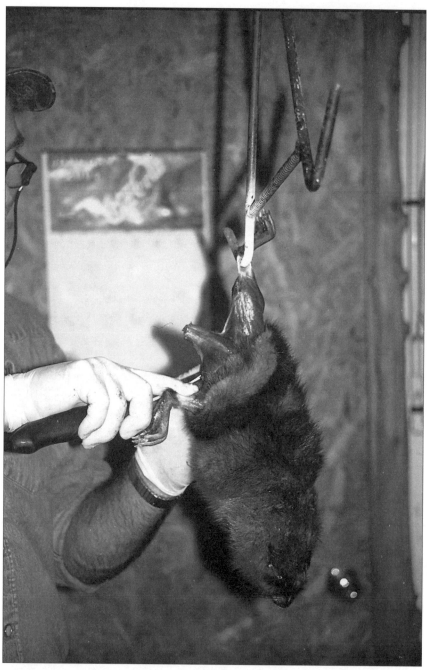

Peel the skin down over the hind legs, using a knife to help free the skin.

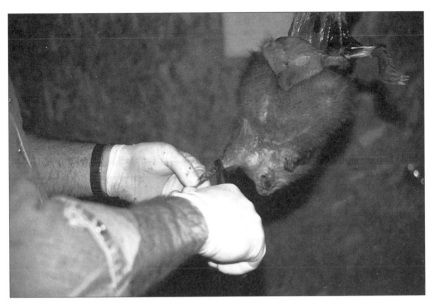

Cut off the front feet.

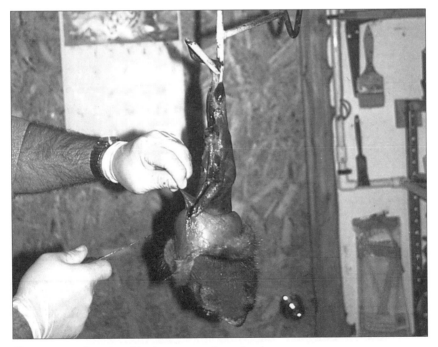

Continue peeling the skin down over the animal.

Once the skin is loosened about halfway down, you can judiciously pull off much of it.

Carefully cut the skin away from the head.

Take special care when skinning out the head to avoid cutting through the skin and ruining the pelt. When you reach the ears, cut behind and through each one, leaving the ears on the pelt. Go extra slowly and carefully as you work down toward the eyes. Cut around both eyes to free the skin. Carefully cut around the lips, then cut off the tip of the nose to leave it with the pelt. Cut away the skin at the bottom of the chin. Many trappers today cut off the bottom lip, because it doesn't add to the pelt's value and often rots.

Open Pelt

Beavers are more commonly skinned with the open-pelt method, and if you wish to keep a coon, muskrat, or woodchuck skin for a wall decoration or any other reason, you can also skin it in this manner. With a beaver, your first step is to cut off all four feet. Then make a straight-line cut along the center of the belly from the base of the tail to the tip of the lower jaw. (On raccoons, leave the feet on, and make a cut from the tip of each foot's heel along the underside of the legs to the centerline cut.) Do not slit the skin on the

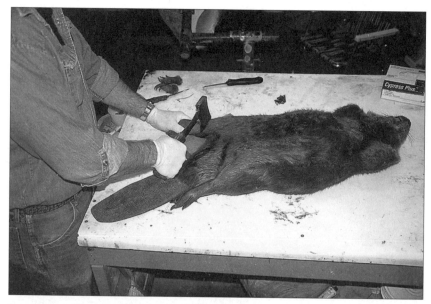

Some animals, particularly beavers, are skinned open pelt. In this case the first step is to cut off the feet.

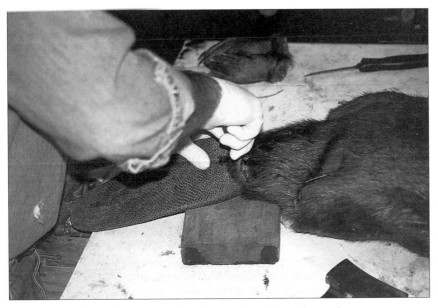

Then cut off the tail by first cutting through the skin and muscle.

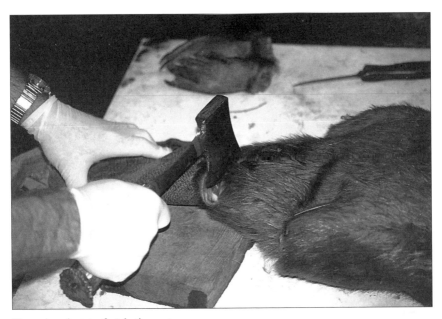

Use a hatchet to finish the cut.

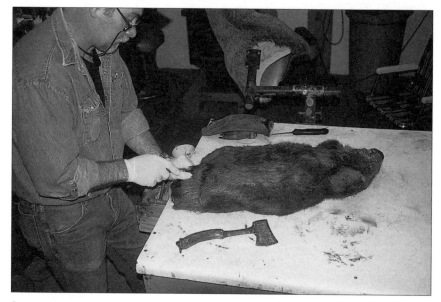

Starting at the tail cut, slice the skin from the underside.

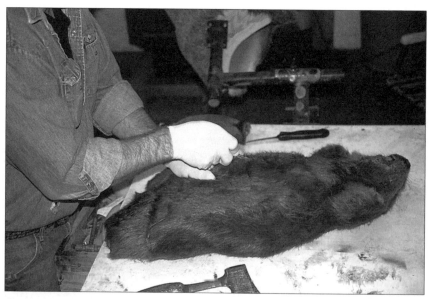

Work the cut all the way up the belly, being careful not to cut into the belly muscle.

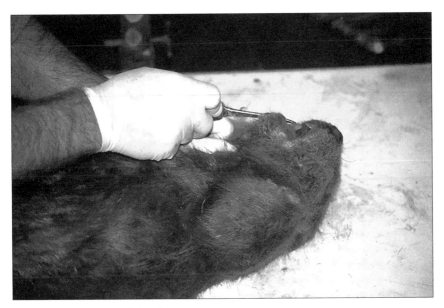

Continue to the tip of the chin.

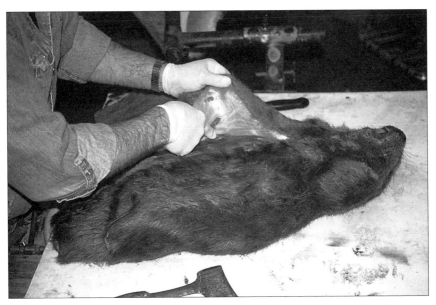

Carefully peel away the skin, cutting with the knife to help loosen the skin.

Make sure you don't cut through the skin—take your time.

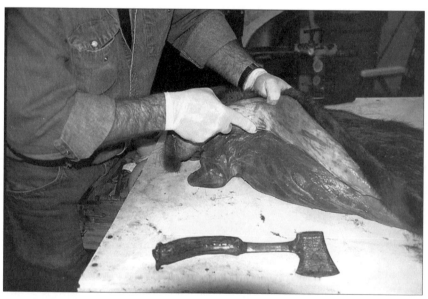

Once the belly side is finished, turn the animal over and work on its back.

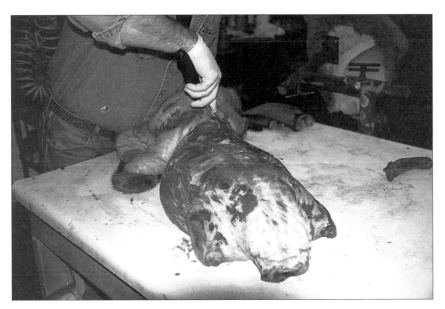

Carefully skin up and over the head.

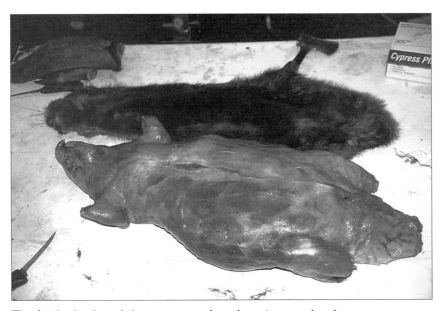

The finished pelt, and the carcass ready to be eviscerated and cut up.

legs of beaver, but cut around the skin at the base of the tail, then cut off the tail. Using a sharp knife to assist you, skin the pelt off the body, down over the legs and head. Make sure you take extra care around the ears, eyes, and skull. Each cut in the pelt lowers its value.

FLESHING

All fat and meat must be removed from the hide by "fleshing." But first, comb the fur to remove any burrs or other objects. Then split the tail (if you haven't already done so) by pushing a knife blade under the skin, blade-out. Position the hide over a fleshing board and use a knife or hide scraper to scrape loose the fat and muscle or meat. Most beginners to this task don't remove enough fat and meat. Even the smallest amount of fat or meat left on the skin can allow the fur to slip. Go all the way down to the hide.

STRETCHING HIDES

The next step is to stretch the hide so it can dry and "cure" properly. Wire stretching frames are available in a variety of sizes, or you can make up your own from ¾-inch-thick wooden planks. The frames or stretchers must fit the pelt correctly. The pelt is not actually stretched in place, but should fit fairly snugly. Pushpins hold the lower end of the pelt in place on the wooden forms. Depending on the animal and temperature, the pelt should dry within anywhere from a few days to a week or so. Remove all grease from the pelt and hang it in a dry, cool place until it can be marketed or tanned. The pelt should be turned right-side-out after it cures.

EVISCERATING

Raccoons, beavers, woodchucks, opossums, and muskrats are all eviscerated in much the same way as rabbits and squirrels. Make a cut in the belly skin to the anal vent, being careful not to cut into the entrails. Then turn the carcass and, with the knife blade up, make a cut through the center bone of the rib cage to the throat.

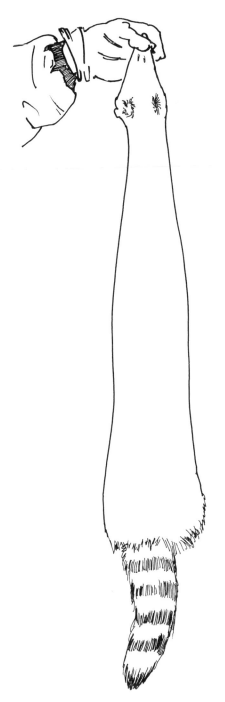

The skin and fur of most small game is often valuable and can easily be preserved.

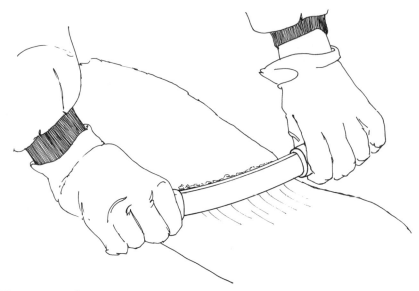

To preserve, all meat and fat left on the skin must be removed by scraping with a fleshing tool.

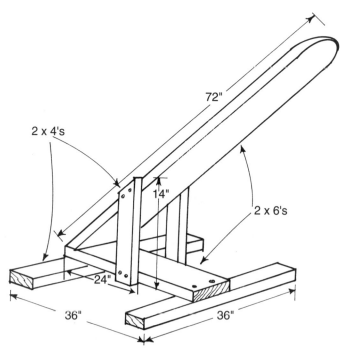

A homemade fleshing beam makes the chore easier.

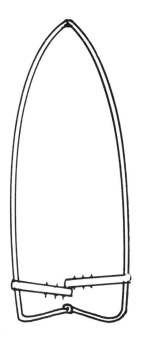 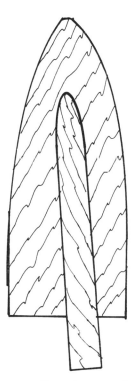

The skin is then placed on a stretcher and allowed to cure. Stretchers can be purchased metal hoops, or homemade from wood.

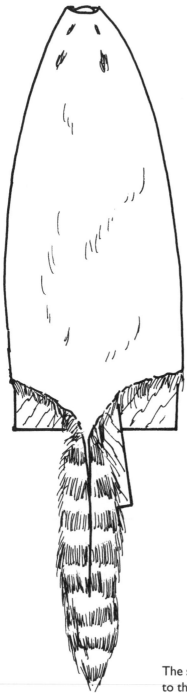

The skin is first stretched inside-out, then turned to the outer side.

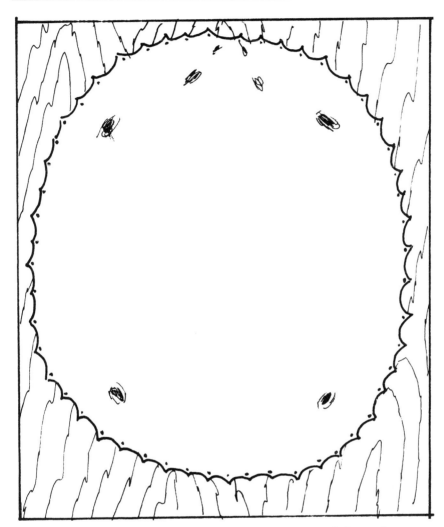

Beaver skins are best stretched by tacking them to a piece of plywood.

Split the pelvis. Then girdle around the genitals and the anal vent, leaving these attached to the viscera. Once this throat-to-vent incision is made, the entire viscera can easily be removed.

CUTTING UP

Smaller animals such as opossums and muskrats can be quartered in the same method you'd use for squirrels or rabbits. Larger animals like raccoons, beavers, and woodchucks can be initially cut into quarters, then into smaller chunks, because they're most often used in stews. You can also debone the meat before cooking if you like.

SCENT GLANDS AND FAT

The meat of many small game animals—in particular raccoons, opossums, beavers, and muskrats—typically has quite a bit of fat, which can be quite rancid. Remove all the fat you can from the leg muscles. Most of these animals also have scent glands located under the forelegs, along with small kernels of scent glands in the small of the back on each side of the backbone. All scent glands must be removed in the dressing process.

Once the carcasses have been skinned and cut up, trim away any shot-damaged meat, wash the carcass in cold water, then place in a freshwater bath with salt added and allow it to soak overnight. This will help take away some of the "gamy" flavor.

Freezing and Canning Small Game

T he steps needed to assure high-quality small game meat do not end at the field-dressing and butchering stage. Proper storage is just as important. Although several methods can be used to preserve meat, including drying, smoking, and canning, the most common method these days is freezing.

While it's simple and effective, freezing is limited in its ability to maintain quality. Freezing protects against immediate spoilage, but affects quality and flavor by freeze-drying the meat. This is especially true in "frost-free" freezers, which pull moisture from the refrigerated air to prevent frost buildup.

PREPARATION

The first step in freezing is to prepare your meat for wrapping. It's important to handle the meat correctly at this stage. Remove all fat from small game—this can often turn rancid even while frozen. Freeze boneless meat intact, rather than sliced ready to fry. Moisture escapes from each cut surface, speeding deterioration. Cut the meat as desired after it has partially thawed, but is still firm enough to slice easily.

WRAPPING

Wrap the meat carefully to maintain quality for as long as possible. Heavy-duty freezer paper or aluminum foil are both equally effective, although foil is easier to use on odd-shaped pieces. Plastic zippered freezer bags are a very convenient way to freeze small game meat. A better method, however, is to double-wrap. First use plastic food wrap, followed by freezer paper, aluminum foil, or a zippered bag. If you're using freezer paper, freezer tape will seal the package together.

Above all, remember to label the packages with their contents and the month and year. You might also want to denote the specific hunting trip: RABBITS IN MISSOURI, for instance, plus the date of the trip. Regardless of how careful I am about labeling, it seems that once or twice a year I pull out a mystery package with no label. What I thought was rabbit once turned out to be duck. It all gets eaten, but it's hard to make hasenpfeffer for guests from duck.

When wrapping meat, squeeze as much air from the package as possible. When small pieces are to be frozen together (such as with young squirrels), the best way to eliminate air is to water pack: Stack the meat pieces in plastic bags or containers, cover with water, and freeze. Once they're frozen, add more water if necessary. Water-packed meat generally lasts longer than standard butcher-wrapped meat.

Another method of water freezing is to glaze-coat the individual pieces of meat and freeze them on open trays. Lay meat pieces on a plastic-wrap-covered tray, mist the top surface with water, and freeze. Then mist spray all surfaces of the meat again, and freeze again before packaging. This will keep the meat pieces separate while they're frozen, much like the large bags of chicken breasts available in the supermarket. If you need only a few pieces for a stew you can remove them, leaving the rest of the meat in the package, undisturbed. This method also provides some extra freezer-burn protection.

STORAGE TIMES

You should plan to use all game within a year of freezing. Not only does this provide the best meat, but it's also often required by game-possession laws. Depending on how the meat is wrapped and what type of freezer you use, quality may remain constant for longer periods. Freezing for longer periods affects taste and quality, but poses no other risks. The following chart gives an approximate storage guide for various cuts of meat.

Meat Type	Maximum Storage
Small game, butcher wrap	8 months
Small game, water pack	12 months
Small game, cut in pieces, butcher wrap	8 months
Whole small game animals (large), butcher wrap	5 months
Whole small game animals (small), butcher wrap	6 months
Whole small game, water pack	12 months

VACUUM PACKING

The ultimate method of preserving by freezing is using a vacuum-packing machine, such as the FoodSaver Professional II, to remove oxygen from the container. Oxidation (exposure to oxygen in the air) is the main cause of food spoilage. When foods absorb oxygen, they begin a process of irreversible chemical change. Contact with oxygen causes foods to lose nutritional value, texture, flavor, and overall quality.

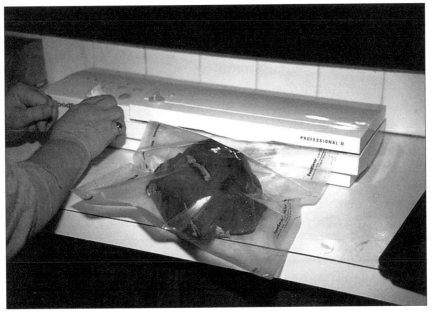

The best method of preserving small game meat is to use a vacuum packer such as the FoodSaver.

Oxygen enables microorganisms such as bacteria, mold, and yeast to grow. These microorganisms cause rapid deterioration of food. Exposure to freezing-cold air also causes "freezer burn" in frozen foods. (Freezer burn is localized dehydration.) Oxygen causes foods that are moderately high in fats and oils to yield a rancid odor and flavor. Air carries moisture, and moisture causes the food to become soggy and lose its texture. Moisture causes "caking" in dry solids, making them difficult to handle. Oxygen also allows insects to survive and hatch.

When oxygen is removed from the storage environment, however, foods can be stored three to five times longer than with conventional storage methods. In the absence of oxygen, dried foods, frozen foods, and perishable foods requiring refrigeration will retain their "just-bought" freshness and flavor much longer—resulting in less food waste.

Preventing air from coming in contact with stored food is a two-step process.

Step 1. Remove all the air currently in the container.
Step 2. Prevent air from reentering the container.

This requires that two conditions be met:

• The container needs to be made of a material that provides a barrier against oxygen.
• The seal on the container needs to be airtight.

Vacuum packaging is the process of removing the air from a container so that a vacuum is created, and then sealing the container so that air cannot reenter.

Vacuum-packaging systems are able to create a vacuum in storage bags, canisters, jars, cans, and bottles. Storage bags used for freezing are specially designed to provide an oxygen and moisture barrier and to maintain an airtight seal. To provide an effective barrier, the bags should be constructed of plastic or a nylon layer. They should also have a pattern of small "air channels" to ensure that air pockets don't form as the air is being removed.

It's important to choose the proper vacuum-packaging system. Bag sealers, sometimes thought of as vacuum-packaging systems, use a heated wire that welds the bag closed. They do not have any mechanism for removing air from the bag before sealing. Some bag sealers come with a small rotary fan that extracts some of the air from the bags before they're sealed. Other systems utilize polyethylene bags. Still others provide sheets of plastic from which bags of different sizes can be made by "welding" the seams with a heated wire bag-sealing mechanism. The fans in these models don't have enough suction to create a vacuum; the process is comparable to using a straw to suck air out of the bag. The plastic will shape itself loosely to the contours of the food in the bag, but it will be obvious that air remains in the bag. The type of bag material, and the strength of the seal, will determine whether oxygen is able to reenter the bag.

Electric-powered vacuum-packaging systems, on the other hand, eliminate exposure to oxygen. These systems extract the air from a variety of containers, including bags. The FoodSaver Professional II uses patented bags.

Once a small package is vacuum packed, it stays fresh in the freezer for up to two years; large cuts of meat will stay fresh up to three years. Also, vacuum-packaged meat takes up less space in the freezer because it doesn't have to be packed in water. I've been testing the FoodSaver Professional II for some time and find it an excellent choice for vacuum packing.

CANNING SMALL GAME

Another way to preserve small game is by pressure canning. Although canning is more time-consuming than quickly freezing your game, canned meats require no electrical power while they're stored, and you don't have to wait for meat to thaw before preparing a meal. The meat is cooked before canning and can also be deboned before canning to save space.

To prepare meat for canning, dress as described for each animal, being sure to remove the scent glands and all fat. Soak the meat overnight as if you're preparing to cook. Then precook until the meat can be separated from the bones, but don't salt the cooking water. Change the cooking water if needed. Drain the meat, debone, and dice. Pack it loosely into pint or quart canning jars, adding ½ teaspoon of salt to each pint jar and 1 teaspoon to each quart jar. Fill the jars with fresh boiled water to within 1 inch of the top, adjust the lids, and process according to the times and pressure recommended by the manufacturer of your canner. *Note:* If your pressure canner is an older model, check with your local County Extension Service office to see if the time and pressure recommended in its booklet meet current standards.

If you haven't previously canned wild game, you might want to try it, at least for a portion of your small game meat. The finished product has not only an interesting taste, but added convenience as well. The canned meat is ready to use in any recipe calling for boned, diced meat.

CHAPTER

6

Smoking and Drying Small Game

Smoking and drying are excellent methods of preserving small game, but they are seldom used today. Small game usually do not result in the abundance of meat that larger game animals provide. Smoking and drying are good options, however, especially for short-term storage and if other types of storage are unavailable. This chapter discusses preserving meat by both cold smoking and hot smoke cooking, as well as drying.

SMALL GAME JERKY

Small game can be dried as jerky, or made into pemmican or summer-type sausage, although other types of meats are more commonly used. Actually jerky can be made of just about any meat; you can even use a "potpourri" of wild game meats to make up jerky, especially if you're using the more modern ground-meat method. You can combine small game, venison, big game, and gamebirds into the same recipe in this manner.

If you do wish to make jerky, following is a quite simple sliced-jerky method. Trim away all fat and as much connective tissue as possible from the meat. Then cut it into strips about ¼ inch thick, cutting *with* the grain rather than across it. Combine the meat with Lawry's Seasoned Marinade or another bottled or packaged marinade in a glass bowl or zippered plastic bag and refrigerate for at least 2 hours.

Or use the following ingredients to make your own marinade:

You can slice small game meat into strip jerky.

You can also grind small game pieces to make ground jerky or sausage.

¼ cup canning or meat salt
¼ cup brown sugar
1 cup soy sauce
1 tablespoon Worcestershire sauce
1 teaspoon garlic powder
1 teaspoon lemon pepper
1 teaspoon onion powder
Tabasco sauce (a few drops or more depending on taste)

Again, combine all these ingredients with your meat in a glass bowl or zippered plastic bag and add water to cover. You can adjust the spices in the above recipe and add flavorings to suit. Wine, bourbon, or brandy can also be used to replace some of the water. If it takes more than about 3 cups of water to cover your meat, increase the spices. Refrigerate for 8 to 12 hours or overnight.

Remove from the refrigerator, shake the excess marinade from the strips, and pat them dry. For spicier jerky, shake dried red pepper flakes or Cajun seasoning onto the meat strips before drying.

To dry the meat, place a sheet of aluminum foil in the bottom of your oven to catch any drippings and drape the meat over the oven racks, leaving enough space between pieces for air to circulate. Spraying the oven racks beforehand with a cooking spray keeps the jerky strips from sticking. Set the oven to 160 degrees or as low as it can be set and then crack the door open an inch or so.

According to the United States Department of Agriculture (USDA) Food Safety and Inspection Service (FSIS), "When raw meat or poultry is dehydrated at home — either in a warm oven or a food dehydrator — to make jerky which will be stored on the shelf, pathogenic bacteria are likely to survive the dry heat of a warm oven and especially the 130° to 140°F of a food dehydrator." Following is their recommended methods of properly drying jerky:

Due to the possibility of illness from Salmonella and E.coli 0157:H7 from homemade jerky, the USDA current recommendation for making jerky safely is to heat meat to 160°F before the dehydrating process. This step assures that any bacteria present will be destroyed by wet heat. But most dehydrator instructions do not include this step, and a dehydrator may not reach temperatures high enough to heat meat to 160°F. After heating to 160°F, maintaining a constant dehydrator temperature of 130° to 140°F during the drying process is important because (1) the process must be fast enough to dry food before it spoils; and (2) it must remove enough water that microorganisms are unable to grow.

The USDA recommends the following safe handling and preparation methods:

— Always wash hands thoroughly with soap and water before and after working with meat products.
— Use clean equipment and utensils.
— Keep meat and poultry refrigerated at 40°F or slightly below; use or freeze ground meats and poultry within 2 days; whole red meats, within 3 to 5 days.
— Defrost frozen meat in the refrigerator, not on the kitchen counter.
— Marinate meat in the refrigerator. Don't save marinade to re-use. Marinades are used to tenderize and flavor the jerky before dehydrating it.
— Steam or roast meat and poultry to 160°F as measured with a meat thermometer before dehydrating it.
— Dry meats in a food dehydrator that has an adjustable temperature dial and will maintain a temperature of at least 130° to 140°F throughout the drying process.

Most jerky will take 5 or 6 hours to dry, but times vary depending on the heat of your oven and the thickness of the meat. Begin checking for doneness after 3 hours, removing the pieces as they become dry.

The jerky should not be pink inside, but don't overdry small game meat. Jerky is done when you can still bend it—overdone when it snaps. Store the finished product in a cool, dry place. Vacuum sealing works well for storing jerky over long periods of time, but the meat's sharp edges tend to cut the bags—wrapping in aluminum foil before packing solves the problem.

Ground Jerky

A better method of making jerky from small game meat is to use ground meat run through a jerky gun, such as those available from Cabela's and Bass Pro. These guns often come in a kit complete with the spices you need to mix with specified pounds of ground meat. This process makes jerky quick and easy. Grinding the meat also allows you to use smaller chunks of meat, which might not be as readily utilized for sliced jerky. The jerky is extruded into strips

To make jerky, mix spices with the ground meat in a stainless steel or plastic bowl and marinate.

Then squeeze the mix through a jerky gun.

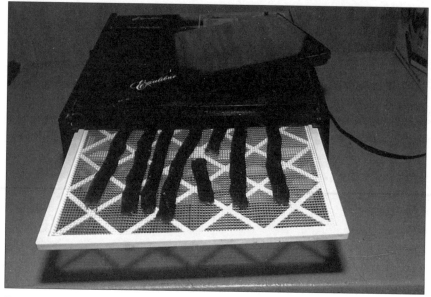

Dry the jerky in an oven or dehydrator.

or rolls, then dried in the same manner as sliced jerky, though the strips have to lie flat. If you're using your oven as the dryer, extrude the strips or rolls onto any food-safe, washable screening, cheesecloth, or parchment paper and lay these on the oven racks to dry.

You can also make up your own ground jerky following the recipe below, but you'll still need a jerky gun to make the jerky strips or rolls.

5 pounds ground small game meat
5 heaping teaspoons Morton Tender Quick Salt
¼ cup brown sugar
1 teaspoon garlic powder
1 teaspoon onion powder
¼–½ teaspoon ground red pepper or ½ teaspoon dried red pepper flakes

Mix the spices, then sprinkle a portion of them over the ground meat and use your hands to blend. Keep adding the spices in batches, mixing well after each addition. Again, the spices and flavorings can be adjusted to suit your taste. As with the marinades, use a stainless-steel, enameled, glass, or plastic container. Cover the container and refrigerate for at least 12 hours or overnight. Then press into jerky strips or rolls and dry as above.

COLD SMOKING

Small game can also be brined and "cold smoked," but the results should still be kept refrigerated or frozen. This technique is rarely done with small game, however. Although cold smoking is a means of preservation, we no longer smoke dry meats for the time required to preserve them without refrigeration. Instead I usually use a cold smoker to begin the process, add smoke flavor, then finish the process in the oven. Cold smoking requires a cold smoker, such as the electric Little Chief Smoker from Luhr-Jensen. This is a simple metal box with racks to hold items for smoking. An electric plate in the bottom provides the heat, and a pan sitting on the plate holds wood chips to provide the smoke.

The Luhr-Jensen Little Chief Smoker can be used for smoking, smoke flavoring, or drying, and comes with a complete instruction book loaded with tasty recipes. The same smoker can be used to cure jerky and smoke sausages. The company also sells a wide assortment of brine and seasoning mixes, including All-Purpose Brine Mix as well as different wood-flavor fuels including hickory, apple, alder, cherry, and mesquite.

You can also make up your own cold smoker from an old refrigerator. I've even used a large wooden box as a cold smoker. Caution: If using a refrigerator as a smoker or for any other purpose, remove the locking device from the door and replace with a simple latch.

You'll also need refrigerator space or a large cooler for the brining process, or you can brine during cold weather as the old-timers did. The brine temperature must be kept below 40 degrees, but not freezing. For this reason it is extremely difficult to do depending only on Mother Nature.

A simple brine consists of:

2 gallons water
1½ cups canning or meat salt
¼ cup granulated sugar

¼ cup brown sugar
1 teaspoon onion powder
1 teaspoon garlic powder
⅓ cup soy sauce

Place the thawed or fresh game in a plastic, ceramic, or glass container and cover with the brine. The game must be kept submerged in the brine. Use a clean dinner plate and a clean weight (such as a plastic bag filled with water) to hold down the meat. Soak the meat in brine for 24 hours; halfway through the process, rearrange the meat and stir the brine to keep it working and ensure that all the meat is brined properly.

Fire up the smoker and bring the temperature up to 110 to 125 degrees. Maintain the temperature at 100 degrees and keep the wood chip supply replenished. It will normally take about 36 hours to properly smoke the meat. To ensure that the meat is cooked through, smoke until its internal temperature reaches 165 degrees on a meat thermometer. This may take quite a bit more time for large pieces.

Another method is to smoke for about 24 hours or until golden brown, then finish in a conventional oven until the desired temperature is reached. The game should be wrapped in aluminum foil and a bit of liquid or water added to avoid overdrying.

SMOKED SUMMER SAUSAGE

One great way to use pieces of small game—or any wild game—is smoked summer sausage. You can have a smokehouse make your sausage, mixing 1 part lean pork with 1 part small game meat. If you have a grinder and cold smoker or smokehouse, though, you can make your own small game summer sausage. The easiest way to do this is with Luhr-Jensen Summer Sausage Seasoning Mix. Mix each package with 5 pounds of ground small game or a small game/lean pork blend, let cure overnight, then stuff into casings and smoke.

To make your own seasoning mix, try the recipe below. Hot spices and other flavorings can also be added to suit. These quantities will season 10 pounds of sausage:

8 pounds small game meat
2 pounds pork

Small game meat can be used in summer-type sausages using a kit like this, which comes with prepared mixes, a stuffer, and casings.

6 tablespoons salt
1 tablespoon black pepper
¼ cup powdered dextrose
1 teaspoon dry mustard
1 teaspoon ground ginger
1 teaspoon ground coriander
2 tablespoons corn syrup solids
1 teaspoon garlic powder

Grind the game and pork through a ³⁄₁₆-inch grinder plate. Mix all the ingredients in a plastic or stainless-steel bowl or container. Cover and place in a refrigerator for 48 hours. Regrind the meat through a ³⁄₁₆-inch grinder plate and stuff it into casings. The most commonly used casings are 2½- to 2¾-inch by 24-inch beef middles.

Hang the sausages on smoke sticks to dry at room temperature for about 5 hours. Preheat your smoker or smokehouse to between 120 and 130 degrees. Place the sausages in the smokehouse and maintain the temperature for 3 to 4 hours. Then raise the temperature to 165 degrees and cook. The internal tempera-

The first step is to mix the meat and spices and let marinate. Then place a casing over the stuffer and put the meat into the stuffer.

Push down the plunger to stuff the casings.

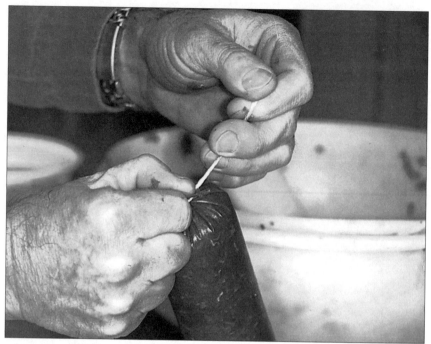

Tie off the sausages.

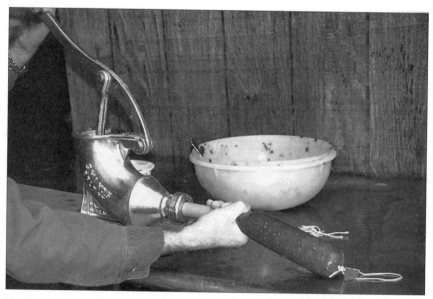

You can also mix your own seasonings and use a sausage stuffer.

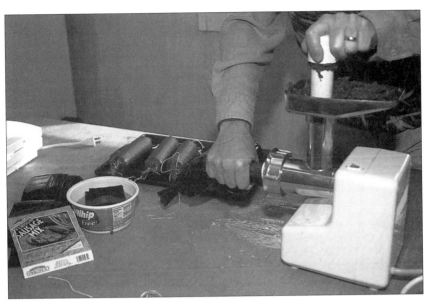

Or you can stuff the sausages with a grinder fitted with a stuffer attachment.

ture of the sausages must reach 165 degrees. When cooking is done, shower the sausages with cold water until their internal temperature drops to 120 degrees. Hang at room temperature for 1 to 2 hours, then place in a cooler for 24 hours. If you don't have a smokehouse capable of reaching these temperatures, you can smoke for the initial flavor, then finish in an oven set at 225 degrees.

Although summer sausage stuffed in purchased casings has a better appearance, sausages can be made without casings. Simply shape the meat into uniform-sized logs and wrap them in cheesecloth or roll in aluminum foil. Puncture foil-wrapped sausages with a fork several times so that the smoke flavoring can penetrate. Tie the ends of the cheesecloth or foil-wrapped rolls, hang them in the smoker, and smoke as above.

To make summer sausage without a smoker, add Liquid Smoke to the sausage mix (½ teaspoon per 5 pounds of meat, or to taste). Cook the sausage in the oven at 225 degrees until the internal temperature reaches 165 degrees.

More information about cold smoking, along with most of the supplies you'll need—including casings, grinders, and stuffers—is

Sausages are placed in a cold smoker.

available from The Sausage Maker. Complete instructions also come with the Luhr-Jensen sausage and brining kits as well as with the Little Chief Electric Smoker from Luhr-Jensen.

SMOKE COOKING AND SMOKE FLAVORING

Smoke cooking, also known as hot smoking, is an excellent method of cooking some small game. Smoke cooking is cooking with high heat while adding smoke at the same time. Smoke cooking or "barbecuing" is a southern tradition. Parked behind many a barn or shed in my part of the Ozarks is a homemade smoker. Today, however, a variety of manufactured cookers and smokers make smoking and smoke cooking easy and reliable.

Three types of "smoke" cookers are available. First is a simple barbecue grill, charcoal or gas. You either pile on the charcoal briquettes or light the gas and cook with the heat. Charcoal adds some smoke flavor; wood chips can also be added to the ignited charcoal, as well as to most gas grills, for extra smoke flavoring.

The second type of smoke cooker uses a high dome with a lid and a separate pan to hold marinade. Moistened wood chips are added for smoking. A number of these units are available commercially, including models from Cabela's, Brinkman, Coleman, and Bass Pro. Both of these smokers cook by direct heat.

True smokers, however, are quite often larger models made of welded metal (to maintain more consistent heat); they're capable of handling much more fire as well as more meat at one loading. These smokers cook by indirect heat, with the coals in one area of the smoker and the meat in another. A number of models are available, but the best I've tested is the Good-One Grill and Smoker from Ron Goodwin Enterprises. The Good-One is available in several sizes, from small to large commercial models, and all are built with the same basic design. The front lower compartment is the firebox and grill. You can grill just as you would with any charcoal grill. The upper back compartment, however, is for smoking or cooking meats with lower, indirect heat. On the lower front of the firebox are the air-control dampers to control the heat in the firebox and grill area. On the top of the smoker lid is an exhaust vent. The heat in the smoker is controlled by the dampers. The smokers are constructed with a cleanout pan located under the firebox grate.

Wood chips are added.

To smoke, remove the top grate from the bottom compartment and place charcoal on the bottom grate. You'll need about 10 pounds of charcoal for several hours of smoking. After the coals are burning, add the wood chunks to provide the smoke flavor and close the bottom lid. As in any smoking, the type of wood chunks used provide the flavoring. These types of smokers do not use water pans. "Water pans make steam heat, which can cause smoke to disappear rapidly and tends to make meat soggy," says Ron Goodwin. "We don't recommend water pans for true, old-fashioned pit barbecue flavor." Ron also suggests using pure charcoal chunks rather than briquettes, although the former are a little harder to obtain. "Another secret to good barbecue smoked meat is a smoker that will hold an even temperature and the right amount and kind of wood," Ron adds. "Hickory, mesquite, oak, pecan, alder, fruit woods—cherry, peach, apple, or grapevine—are recommended. Poultry requires much less wood than other meats, and gamebirds and waterfowl are very good if smoked using fruit woods. The best result for smoke flavor is to use chunks of wood; two or three chunks, about 3 to 4 inches in size, usually give a nice smoked flavor." Small game is best smoked in hickory or mesquite.

The sausages are smoked to give them flavor, then finished in the oven.

Smallgame can be cold or hot smoked, using a variety of smokers.

Maintaining an even temperature over a long period of time is important for ease in smoke cooking. The Good-One smoker has a temperature gauge and a variety of ways to regulate the heat. By simply opening and closing the dampers you can control the heat precisely. You'll also need a meat thermometer to check the internal temperature of your meat.

Smoke cooking does help keep the moisture in the meat rather than drying it out. Ron Goodwin suggests the following for hot smoking with his unit. "Cook 50 to 60 minutes per pound at a temperature of 225 to 250 degrees. When done, baste with sauce, cut the temperature back to 150, and hold for serving. If you don't serve within an hour, wrap in foil."

I prefer to smoke for an hour or two, then wrap the meat in foil for the remainder of the cooking process. This tends to hold in more moisture. The meat can be basted with barbecue sauce, left natural, or basted with lemon pepper and butter or a marinade of your choice.

Smoking small game is fun. The meat can be eaten hot from the smoker; they also make great hors d'oeuvres and cold snacks.

7

Cooking Small Game

Most small game is fairly lean, although some of the critters do carry quite a lot of fat, especially in the winter months. The fat, however, is not in the form of marbling, but usually layered under the skin. As with all game, removing excess fat is a first step in preparing for the table. Make sure all blood, damaged meat, and shot are also removed. It's also just good common sense to make sure the meat is kept clean and properly cooled to maintain freshness and provide safe food.

Small game can be baked, fried, broiled, boiled, grilled, or cooked in a slow cooker, although some techniques are more suited to certain meats than others. Some small game requires little in the way of flavoring; other kinds get a little help from marinades and flavored sauces or spices.

Domestic meat animals are preconditioned by proper feeding to assure the same "quality" of eating that we've come to expect. Small game animals, on the other hand, are quite often what they eat. For the most part these critters—including squirrels, rabbits, groundhogs, and even raccoons—are primarily vegetarians, though raccoons are omnivorous, meaning they'll eat insects, other small animals, fish, crawfish, and more. The condition of the animal is extremely important. It may be fat, lean, healthy, or unhealthy. Do not eat the meat from small game animals that are noticeably unhealthy, diseased, crippled, or don't act right.

The age of the animal is also crucial. Young animals are preferred, although it's usually hard to discern age when hunting. All wild game is best eaten while fresh, and proper care should be taken to field dress and maintain freshness.

RABBIT

Rabbit meat is white, quite comparable to chicken. Most of your favorite chicken recipes can be prepared with rabbit; you must, however, cook according to the rabbit's age. While most of the chicken available today is young and tender and can be used in any recipe, your rabbit may be old and tough and suitable only for stewing or baking.

Rabbit Fricassee

1 rabbit, cleaned and cut into serving-sized pieces
Salt and pepper

Flour

Oil

1 10¾-ounce can cream of mushroom soup

1 soup can milk (use part sour cream, if desired)

Salt and pepper each piece of rabbit, and roll it in flour. Brown both sides in ¼ inch of oil in a cast-iron skillet or Dutch oven with a lid. After browning, smother the meat in the soup stirred together with the milk and cover. Place in a 350-degree oven for approximately 1 hour or until tender. Add more milk or water if it gets too dry.

Smothered Rabbit

This recipe comes from my good friend Ed (Scrappy) Dobbins, a longtime hunting buddy.

6 tablespoons soy sauce

Dash hot pepper sauce, or to taste

½ teaspoon black pepper

1 teaspoon paprika

1 teaspoon dried basil

2- to 3-pound rabbit, cut in pieces

3 tablespoons olive oil

¾ cup flour

2 cups finely sliced onions

1 cup dry white wine

1 cup beef stock

1 teaspoon salt

1 teaspoon minced garlic

½ cup minced fresh parsley

Combine the first five ingredients in a glass bowl. Add the rabbit, rubbing each piece with the mixture. Let marinate from 1 hour to overnight. Heat the oil in a high-sided, ovenproof skillet or Dutch oven. Coat the rabbit pieces lightly with flour, shaking off the excess. Brown them in the hot oil, turning frequently, for 5 to 6 minutes. Remove the rabbit pieces.

Preheat the oven to 350 degrees. Add the onions to the skillet and cook over low heat until softened. Increase the heat to medium, add the wine, and stir to mix all the cooking juices. Return the rabbit to the skillet, then add the beef stock, salt, garlic, and parsley. Mix well and turn the rabbit pieces to coat with the sauce. Cover the skillet and place it in the oven. Cook until the rabbit is tender, about 1 hour, stirring occasionally. Serve with mashed potatoes or rice.

Marinated Rabbit

Cut a rabbit into serving-sized pieces and marinate 24 to 48 hours in a glass or enameled container in the following ingredients:

1 cup water
1 cup claret
1 large onion, diced
2 cups wine vinegar
1 teaspoon mustard seeds
8 whole cloves
6 bay leaves
1 teaspoon crushed juniper berries or 2 ounces gin
1 tablespoon salt
1 teaspoon black pepper

Remove the rabbit pieces from the marinade, pat them dry, and shake them in some flour. Fry in oil just until they're well browned on all sides, then drain the fat from the skillet. Strain the marinade, add 1 tablespoon sugar (if desired), and pour this over the rabbit. Bring the mixture to a boil, cover tightly, and simmer for about 40 minutes or until the meat is tender. Thicken the broth for gravy by mixing a little flour with melted butter and stirring this into the broth.

Hare Pie

1 medium rabbit, cut up

Soak the rabbit in salt water overnight, then rinse it and place it in a stockpot. Cover with cold water, add salt and pepper, and simmer until the meat is tender. Strain the broth and reserve. Separate the meat from the bones, dicing it into ½-inch chunks.

2 medium potatoes, peeled and diced
1 16-ounce package frozen mixed vegetables or frozen peas and carrots
1 10 ¾-ounce can cream of chicken soup
2 cups baking mix
¾ cup milk

Cover the potatoes with the reserved broth and simmer until tender. Cook the vegetables in reserved broth. Mix the chopped meat, cooked potato chunks, and vegetables. Stir in the cream of chicken soup and pour into a casserole dish. In a separate bowl, stir the milk into the baking mix and drop by spoonfuls over the casserole. Flatten and spread slightly with the back of a spoon. Bake in a 350-degree oven until the casserole is bubbly and the biscuit top browned.

Rabbit Chunks

Debone the meat from 1 young, tender rabbit, then dice the meat into bite-sized pieces. Soak the meat pieces for several hours or overnight in buttermilk. Salt and pepper the meat pieces, then roll them in flour. Fry outside in a fish fryer or inside in an electric deep fryer. Serve with barbecue sauce or your favorite dipping sauce.

Rabbit Stew

2 rabbits, quartered
1 onion, quartered
2 stalks celery, quartered
6 or more peppercorns
Salt

Place all the ingredients into a large stockpot and cover with water. Simmer until the rabbits are tender and the meat easily separates from the bones. Strain the broth, discarding the vegetables, and debone and chop the rabbit into ½-inch cubes. *Note:* At this point, it's easy to refrigerate the broth and deboned, chopped meat and finish preparing the stew the following day. If you do refrigerate the broth overnight, remove all fat from the surface of the broth before continuing.

1 quart cooking broth
6 carrots, scraped and sliced or diced
4 medium potatoes, peeled and diced
4 stalks celery, diced
1 large onion, diced

Place the broth in a large, heavy-bottomed pan and add the carrots. Simmer for 15 minutes, then add next three ingredients and cook until all are tender. Add more broth if needed. Stir in the chopped rabbit. Add:

1 can whole-kernel corn
1 can peas
1 can lima beans, hominy, green beans, or vegetables to suit your family

Simmer together for at least half an hour to blend the flavors, then add salt, pepper, and Tabasco sauce to taste. Thicken slightly with 1 to 2 tablespoons of flour blended in water, broth, vegetable juice, or butter. Serve with crackers, with hot homemade bread slices, or over hot biscuits.

Hasenpfeffer

2 rabbits, cut into serving pieces
1 large onion, diced
2 tablespoons mixed pickling spices
1 tablespoon lemon pepper
1 tablespoon salt
1 clove garlic, chopped
Several drops Tabasco sauce
⅓ cup brown sugar
White vinegar
Water

Place the rabbit pieces in a glass, stainless-steel, or enameled container. Layer the rabbit with the onion and spices and cover with a mixture of 1 part white vinegar and 1 part water. Cover and refrigerate for 24 hours, stirring several times; keep the meat under the vinegar/water mixture at all times. (Weight down the meat with a clean dinner plate and tightly closed water-filled plastic bag if necessary.) Strain the liquid and reserve.

Pat dry the rabbit pieces, coat them with flour, and brown them in oil in a heavy Dutch oven or skillet. Pour some of the reserved liquid over the browned rabbit until it's almost covered. Cover the skillet and simmer until the rabbit is tender, or transfer it to a covered roaster and bake in a 350-degree oven until tender. Adjust the seasonings as needed, and thicken by stirring 1 heaping tablespoon of flour in a little reserved liquid.

South-of-the-Border Rabbit

1 rabbit (or 2 squirrels), simmered in salted water until the meat falls from the bones, deboned, and chopped
1 onion, chopped and sautéed in butter until transparent
1 teaspoon chili powder
1 can (14½ ounces) tomatoes and green chilies, mild or hot
1 teaspoon garlic salt
2 cans (10¾ ounces each) cream of chicken soup (do not dilute)
1 package corn or flour tortillas
½ pound grated cheddar cheese or grated cheddar/Monterey jack combination

Mix the meat with the next five ingredients. Place a layer of tortillas in the bottom of a greased 9- by 13-glass baking dish. Follow with a layer of half of the meat mixture and half of the cheese. Add another layer of tortillas, followed by the rest of the meat mixture, and top with the cheese. Bake at 350 degrees until the cheese is melted and the mixture is heated through.

Rabbit Casserole

1 can (10¾ ounces) cream of celery soup
1 can (10¾ ounces) golden mushroom soup
1 soup can milk
1 cup instant rice
1 rabbit, cleaned and cut into serving pieces
1 package onion soup mix

Mix the celery and mushroom soups together with the milk. Spread the rice in the bottom of a well-greased 9- by 13-inch baking dish or covered roaster. Place the rabbit pieces over the rice. Sprinkle the dry onion soup mix over the rabbit pieces and pour the soup/milk mix over the meat and rice. Cover tightly and bake at 300 degrees for 2 hours or until the rabbit is tender. A young rabbit could be baked at 350 degrees for 1 hour or until tender.

Hawaiian Rabbit
½ cup flour
1 teaspoon salt
1 teaspoon paprika

½ teaspoon ground black pepper
½ cup butter
1 rabbit, cut into serving pieces

Sift together the first four ingredients. Melt the butter and pour it into a 9- by 13-inch baking dish. Brush the butter up around the sides to coat the dish. Pat dry the rabbit pieces, dip them in the melted butter, and then in the flour mix. Place in the baking dish and bake at 350 degrees for 30 to 45 minutes or until rabbit has formed an oven-fried coating.

Mix together:

½ cup catsup
1 cup crushed pineapple with juice
1 teaspoon onion powder
½ teaspoon garlic powder
½ teaspoon dried parsley flakes
2 tablespoons brown sugar

Pour the sauce over the rabbit, cover tightly, and bake at 325 degrees for 1 hour or until tender. Remove the cover, baste the rabbit with sauce, and bake uncovered for 15 minutes more to glaze the rabbit.

Traditional Hasenpfeffer

2 Rabbits
Water
Vinegar
6 Bay leaves
Salt and pepper
2 Onions, sliced

Clean rabbits and cut into serving pieces. Place in a glass, enamel, or plastic container and cover with equal parts vinegar and water. Add the bay leaves, salt, pepper, and onion slices. Cover and refrigerate at least 12 hours. Remove rabbit from marinade and pat dry.

Flour
Salt and pepper
Oil
2 cups strained marinade

Coat the rabbit pieces with seasoned flour and brown in a large Dutch oven. Add the strained marinade, cover the pan, and bake in a 325-degree oven for 1 hour or until the meat is tender. Add more marinade if needed.

2 cups dairy sour cream, regular or low fat
10 to 12 Gingersnaps, crushed

Carefully remove the rabbit pieces to a warm platter. Stir the sour cream and gingersnaps into the pan drippings, heat through, and pour over the rabbit.

Rabbit Fajitas

One rabbit
Italian salad dressing
½ to 2 teaspoons crushed red pepper

Clean one rabbit and soak overnight in salt water. Debone the rabbit meat, cut into strips, and place in a resealable plastic bag or covered dish. Blend the Italian dressing with crushed red pepper flakes to taste and reserve ½ cup marinade for the vegetables. Pour the rest of the marinade over the rabbit meat and marinate overnight.

½ to 1 sweet green pepper
½ to 1 sweet red pepper
½ to 1 sweet yellow pepper
1 onion diced
1 tablespoon oil
Flour tortillas, warmed

In a large, non-stick skillet, sauté the drained rabbit strips in oil. Cut the peppers into lengthwise strips, dice the onion, and toss with the ½ cup reserved marinade. When the meat is browned, add the onions and peppers along with their marinade. Brown and serve in the warm flour tortillas. Note: This can also be grilled in a grill top basket.

Rabbit Alfredo

One rabbit
Red wine or red wine vinegar

Soak a cleaned rabbit overnight in salt water. Debone and dice into ½-inch pieces. Marinate the diced rabbit several hours or overnight in red wine. Marinate in a resealable plastic bag or in a glass, enamel, or plastic covered container.

Oil
1 cup sliced broccoli
1 cup sliced carrots
1 cup sliced cauliflower, or 1 frozen package California mix (carrots, broccoli, and cauliflower)
1 cup diced onion
½ cup diced sweet red pepper
1 1-pound jar Alfredo sauce

Steam the vegetables until tender crisp. If using the frozen California mix, thaw in a colander under cold running water, then drain well. In a large, non-stick sauté pan, sauté the onion in oil until transparent, add the drained rabbit meat, and cook until brown and tender. Add the red pepper and vegetables. Brown all, trying not to break up the vegetables. When all is tender, pour over the Alfredo sauce and warm. Serve over fettuccini.

Rabbit Stew

1 Rabbit
Flour
Salt and pepper
Oil
1 1.25-ounce package Country Gravy Mix
1 1-pound package frozen stew vegetables

Clean rabbit and soak overnight in salt water. Debone and cut the meat into ½-inch cubes. Place the flour, salt, and pepper in a resealable plastic bag or small paper sack. Add the meat chunks a few at a time and shake. Brown in oil in a heavy Dutch oven. Remove the pieces to a warm platter as they brown. Drain the excess oil from the pan. Use a spatula to scrape the pan drippings and stir seasoned flour into the drippings. Mix the Country Gravy Mix with two cups water and add.

Stir and cook over medium heat until a smooth gravy forms. If too thick, add a bit more water. Return the browned meat chunks to the gravy and cook over low heat until tender. Note: The meat and gravy can also be placed in the oven or in an electric slow cooker. When the meat is tender, add the stew vegetables and cook at least another 30 minutes.

Quesadillas

1 Rabbit
1 Onion
2 to 3 whole jalapenos, depending on taste
Salt and pepper

Place the cleaned rabbit in a stew pot, cover with water, and add the vegetables, salt, and pepper. Simmer until the meat falls from the bones. Debone and dice meat. If desired, the meat can now be refrigerated or frozen and the Quesadillas made later.

Diced rabbit meat
Monterey Jack cheese, shredded
Flour tortillas
Oil
Refried beans
Chopped green chilies or other peppers to suit
Salsa

Warm one flour tortilla at a time in a skillet brushed with oil or sprayed with cooking spray. Warm tortilla on both sides until pliable, then place beans, rabbit meat, and cheese on one half of the tortilla and fold the other half over. Grill each Quesadilla about 2 minutes per side or until filling is warm and the cheese melts. Cut each in quarters or wedges depending on the size of the tortilla. Serve with salsa, fresh or bottled. Quesadillas make a great appetizer if cut in small wedges or a main course if cut into larger wedges.

Enchilada Casserole

1 Rabbit
1 Onion
2 to 3 whole jalapenos, depending on taste
Salt and pepper

Place the cleaned rabbit in a stew pot, cover with water, and add the vegetables, salt, and pepper. Simmer until the meat falls from the bones. Debone and dice meat. Note, at this point the meat can be refrigerated or frozen and the casserole made later. The pre-peared casserole can also be frozen.

12 corn tortillas
Shredded cheese, cheddar and Monterey Jack
Diced rabbit meat
Diced onion, chili peppers and sweet peppers
Enchilada sauce, bottled or package mix made according to
  instructions

Stir a little of the enchilada sauce into the rabbit meat, just to moisten. Dip each tortilla in the heated enchilada sauce to soften. Place meat, onions, peppers, and cheese down the center of each tortilla. Roll and place seam side down in a greased baking dish. Top with the remaining sauce and sprinkle with cheese. Bake at 350 degrees for 30 to 45 minutes. Serve topped with shredded lettuce and diced tomatoes.

Country Style Rabbit

2 Rabbits
Salt and pepper
Flour
1 Onion
Celery leaves
6 slices hickory smoked bacon

Cut two cleaned rabbits into serving pieces. Salt and pepper each piece and roll in flour. Place the rabbit in a single layer in a large roaster. Cut the onion into thin slices and spread over the rabbit. Chop the leaves and tops from one package of celery (or dice 3 or 4 stalks celery) and spread over the onion slices. Lay the bacon strips on top. Add water to cover the meat, cover tightly, and place in a 325-degree oven for approximately 3 hours or until the rabbit is ten-der. Great with mashed potatoes and biscuits.

SQUIRREL

Squirrel meat is also white, but not quite as light as rabbit. Although chicken and rabbit recipes can be prepared with squirrel, a number

of specialty squirrel recipes make the most of this favorite small game animal.

Fried Squirrel

Cut a young squirrel into serving-sized pieces and soak them overnight in Italian salad dressing or your favorite vinegar and oil dressing. Drain, but do not pat dry. Shake the pieces in a paper or plastic bag in salt-and-pepper-seasoned flour and fry in a cast-iron skillet in ½-inch of oil. Brown quickly on both sides, then turn down the heat and cook until tender and the juices run clear. Remove from the skillet and make a flour-and-water gravy from the pan drippings.

Note: If you're frying an older squirrel, parboil it first to tenderize. You can also sprinkle it with meat tenderizer before flouring, but a young squirrel is still best for frying.

Deep-Fried Squirrel

Clean and cut into serving-sized pieces several young squirrels. Dip each piece in evaporated milk and then into salt-and-pepper-seasoned flour. Place the dipped pieces on waxed-paper-lined trays. Place the filled trays in the refrigerator for half an hour, then dip and flour each piece again. Again, return to the refrigerator for half an hour then dip again if you like extra-crispy coating. Fry a few pieces at a time in an outdoor fish cooker or other deep fryer.

Brunswick Stew

This recipe for Brunswick Stew comes from the late E. Ragland Dobbins and is still a specialty of his son, Scrappy. This is a large recipe that freezes well.

4 squirrels, cleaned and disjointed
1 large onion, diced
1 tablespoon butter
2 16-ounce packages baby lima beans
2 16-ounce packages whole-kernel corn
2 16-ounce packages okra
2 14½-ounce cans diced tomatoes
1 small bottle Worcestershire sauce
Cayenne pepper
Salt and pepper

Cook the squirrels in salted water until the meat falls from the bones. Debone and dice the meat, straining and saving the cooking liquid. Sauté the onion in the butter until light brown. Place the diced meat, onion, and vegetables into a large, heavy-bottomed pan. Stir in the Worcestershire sauce and some of the cooking liquid. Add a dash of cayenne pepper (or more if you like) and salt and pepper to taste. Cook for about 5 hours over very low heat, stirring often to keep the mixture from sticking. Add cooking liquid as needed. Rag's original southern recipe says, "Simmer until it becomes so thick you can eat with a fork."

Baked Squirrel

This recipe is good for any tough old squirrel or rabbit that isn't suited to other recipes.

Cut up squirrels and soak them for 24 to 48 hours in equal parts of vinegar and water. As always, be sure to marinate in a glass or enameled container. Drain and pat dry. Coat each piece with seasoned flour and brown on both sides in a little oil. Place the meat in a casserole dish. Stir a little flour into the pan drippings, along with 1 package of dry onion soup mix. Add 2 cups of hot water and stir to blend. Blend in 1 10¾-ounce can of cream of chicken soup and pour over the meat. Add more water if necessary to cover the meat. Cover tightly and bake at 325 degrees for at least 1 hour or until tender, adding more water if needed.

Cashew Squirrel

Debone 2 squirrels (or 1 rabbit) and chop the meat into bite-sized pieces. Marinate overnight in soy sauce. Roll the pieces in flour (or cornstarch) and deep fry. Set the meat aside and keep warm.

2 cups chicken broth
2–3 tablespoons oyster sauce
1 tablespoon cornstarch
¼–½ cup unsalted cashew nuts
½ cup sliced green onions

Heat the chicken broth and stir in the oyster sauce. Thicken with cornstarch dissolved in a little water. Stir in some of the cashew nuts.

To serve, place the squirrel pieces over a bed of warm rice, spoon sauce over the meat, and garnish each serving with more cashew nuts and sliced green onions.

Squirrel Stew

Clean and cut up 1 or 2 squirrels. Place them in a slow cooker with 1 medium onion, quartered, and 2 rough-chopped stalks of celery. Cover with water, adding 1 teaspoon of salt for each quart of water. Add ground pepper or peppercorns. Simmer in the slow cooker until the meat falls from the bones.

Pick the meat from the bones and strain the broth into a 4-quart heavy pan. Add diced carrots and potatoes and cook until tender. Add the diced meat and 2 to 3 cans of your favorite vegetables. Thicken slightly with flour and water, or stir in a can of cream of mushroom soup. This recipe will make even the toughest old red tender.

Enchilada Pie

1 large package corn chips (Frito's)
2 squirrels, simmered in salted water until the meat falls from the
  bones, deboned, and chopped
1 large can enchilada sauce or 2 envelopes enchilada sauce mix
  made according to package directions
1 10¾-ounce can cream of mushroom soup, undiluted
1 onion, chopped and sautéed in butter until transparent
½ teaspoon garlic powder
1 16-ounce package grated cheese

Grease a 9- by 13-inch glass baking dish and line it with corn chips
slightly crushed. In a separate bowl, mix the squirrel meat with the
sauce, soup, onion, and garlic. Add salt and pepper to taste. Pour the
meat mixture carefully over the corn chips and sprinkle with cheese.
Add a top layer of corn chips and garnish with cheese. Bake in a
350-degree oven until the dish is bubbly and the cheese is melted.

Busy-Day One-Dish Meal

1 tablespoon oil
1 green pepper, chopped
1 onion, diced
½ teaspoon garlic powder or 1 clove garlic, minced
Salt and pepper
1½–2 cups chopped squirrel or rabbit meat
2 14½-ounce cans diced tomatoes
1 cup uncooked pasta
Parmesan cheese

Heat the oil in a large, heavy skillet with a lid or a Dutch oven. Brown
the pepper, onion, and garlic. Stir in salt and pepper to taste, the
chopped meat, the tomatoes with their juices, and the pasta. Cover
tightly and simmer for 15 to 20 minutes or until the pasta is tender. Stir
occasionally to keep the pasta from sticking. Sprinkle cheese over the
top and serve with a salad. *Note:* Diced tomatoes with green chilies,
diced tomatoes with garlic, or one can of each can be used.

Squirrel Under Sauerkraut

This recipe is from Jerry Thies, a retired doctor form Osceola, Missouri, an avid squirrel and bird hunter and a pretty good cook.

3 or 4 squirrels, cleaned and cut into serving pieces
Flour, seasoned with salt, pepper, and garlic powder
Olive oil
2 or 3 cans sauerkraut, German or American
2 tablespoons brown sugar

Shake the squirrel pieces in the seasoned flour and brown in olive oil. Place the browned squirrel into a casserole or Dutch oven with a tight lid. Spread the sauerkraut and juice over the squirrel in a solid layer and sprinkle the brown sugar over the kraut. Cover with a tight-fitting lid and place in a 300-degree oven for approximately 3 hours or until tender.

Dinner in a Pot

2 cups boned squirrel meat
Flour
Salt and pepper
1 cup diced onion
½ cup diced red or green sweet pepper
½ cup diced celery
Oil
1 1-pound package frozen country fries
1 can tomato soup
½ soup can water
½ cup shredded cheddar cheese

Cut the meat into ½-inch cubes and coat each piece with seasoned flour. Brown in oil. Brown the onion, peppers, and celery. Place in a slow cooker or Dutch oven. Spread the frozen fries over the meat, sprinkle with garlic salt and pepper. Mix the tomato soup with the water and pour over all. Cover tightly and bake in a 350-degree oven for 1 hour; or cook on low in a slow cooker for several hours. Garnish each serving with a little shredded cheese.

RACCOON

Typically raccoons weigh between 12 and 16 pounds when mature. The most common hunting method is following hounds at night, and it's a long-lived tradition in many parts of the country. Raccoons are also taken regularly with predator calls, especially in the evening or nighttime hours where allowed. Trapping is another very common method of taking raccoons. With the recent decrease in fur prices, raccoons, like many furred small game species, have proliferated. In fact, their main habitat may no longer be the mountains of the South and Southeast, as well as the corn country of the Midwest, but cities and towns across the country. Urban and suburban raccoons are definitely on the rise—to the point of being a real nuisance in many areas. Raccoons can carry rabies, a serious threat. Do not dress or eat any animal that doesn't seem healthy and at least somewhat wary.

The taste and texture of raccoon meat can vary a great deal depending mostly on the age of the animal. Raccoon meat is dark and somewhat stringy, without a lot of fat or marbling running through it. Raccoons, however, do tend to have a lot of fat covering the outside of the muscle, and this should all be removed. Younger animals are preferred. As many an Ozarker has discovered, you just about can't boil an old boar coon enough—and even then the broth may be strong enough to walk across.

Raccoons must be dressed carefully. Never allow the hide to touch the meat while skinning, and remove as much fat as possible from the meat. Take extra care to remove the kernel-shaped glands found in the muscles under the arms and between the legs. Soak dressed coon overnight in either salt or soda water or both.

Barbecued Coon

Prepare coon as discussed above, soaking overnight in soda water. Rinse it thoroughly and cut it into serving-sized pieces. Boil in lightly salted water until it's tender, changing the water at least once if you're cooking an older coon. Drain, discarding the cooking water. Place the pieces into a shallow baking pan and brush with your favorite barbecue sauce, bottled or homemade. Bake in a 350-degree oven for approximately 30 minutes or until the meat is well glazed with sauce.

Barbecued Raccoon

Barbecued coon is a favorite with many trappers and hunters. This version comes from Ozarkian Tad Brown, expert trapper and pro hunter with M.A.D.D. Call Company.

1 raccoon, whole or cut into pieces
2 ribs celery

1 onion
Salt
Cooking spray
1 teaspoon Liquid Smoke
½ teaspoon dry mustard
2 tablespoons brown sugar
1 cup barbecue sauce

Parboil the coon with the celery, salt, and onion until tender. Remove the excess fat and bones, discarding the vegetables and broth. Spray a covered baking dish with cooking spray and add the meat. Mix the Liquid Smoke, dry mustard, and brown sugar into the barbecue sauce and pour over the meat. Cover and bake at 300 degrees for 2 hours.

Baked Coon with Dressing

Prepare coon as discussed above, soaking it overnight in soda water. Rinse it thoroughly and cut it into serving-sized pieces. Boil in lightly salted water until it's tender, changing the water if you're cooking an older coon. Drain, discarding the cooking water. Debone and chop the meat into 1-inch pieces. Make up your favorite dressing recipe or prepare two packages stuffing mix. One package cornbread and one package pork stuffing mix make a good combination. Spread the prepared dressing over the bottom of a roasting pan that's coated with oil or cooking spray. Place the meat pieces over the dressing and cover with a can of cream of mushroom soup diluted with ½ cup of milk and ½ cup of sour cream. Make sure all meat pieces are covered with the soup mixture. Bake in a 350-degree oven for 30 minutes or until it's brown and bubbly.

Baked Raccoon

This version of baked raccoon is also from Tad Brown.

1 raccoon, cut into pieces, glands removed
Salt and pepper
Flour
Buttermilk
Oil
Cooking spray

Parboil the coon in salted water until it's tender. Remove and cool. Remove the excess fat. Coat the meat with flour, dip it in buttermilk, and coat it in flour again. Brown on both sides in oil over medium heat. Remove to a covered dish coated with cooking spray, adding salt and pepper to taste. Bake at 300 degrees for 2 hours.

Coon and Sweet Potatoes

1 Raccoon
6 Sweet potatoes
6 tablespoons brown sugar

Clean and cut coon into serving-sized pieces. Soak the cut-up coon in salt and soda water overnight. Drain and rinse the meat. Place in clean, salted water and cook until tender. Peel the sweet potatoes and cut into 2- to 3-inch chunks. Parboil the sweet potatoes in salted water until almost tender. Place the meat in a baking dish or roaster interspersed with the sweet potatoes and some of the potato water. Sprinkle the brown sugar over the meat and sweet potatoes and bake one hour at 300 degrees.

OPOSSUM

The opossum, that legendary southern "slinker," is also expanding its range and habitat these days, finding a home in the pet-food barrels of suburban garages as well as in other areas of "easy pickings." Opossums usually range from 5 to 10 pounds in weight, depending on their age and sex. Very few hunters go out specifically to hunt opossums due to the fact they're primarily nocturnal. In most instances bagged opossums are the result of coon hounds chasing an animal up a tree, this to the disgust of purist houndsmen. Other hunters don't mind the occasional opossum meal. Opossums are fairly easily trapped in both live traps and others, and were a very common problem on my rabbit trapline when I was a kid, although not quite as much as the occasional stray cat or skunk.

Possums tend to be "greasy" or carry quite a lot of fat, intermingled with the muscle, which makes them somewhat difficult to cook properly. Their meat is definitely an acquired taste. My grandmother would bake an occasional opossum, but it was usually more of a "necessity" than a preferred food.

Possums are usually skinned by the methods listed in Chapter 4. The old-fashioned way to dress opossum, however, was by scraping. To dress, an animal should be immersed in very hot water (not boiling) for a minute or two and the hair removed by scraping, similar to dressing a hog. Do this with a knife held flat, or use a hog scraper. Try to scrape without cutting the skin. Redip in hot water if the animal gets so cool that the hair will no longer scrape off easily. Singe if needed.

Regardless of the dressing method, trim all fat and wash inside and out with hot water. Soak overnight in salt water, then rinse again with hot water.

Possum and Sweet Potatoes

1 possum, scraped and soaked overnight in salt water

Parboil the possum in salt water until tender. Discard the cooking water. Place the possum (cut into serving-sized pieces) into a roaster that has been coated with cooking spray. Place scrubbed (but unpeeled) sweet potatoes around the meat. Add salt and pepper and bake at 350 degrees until the sweet potatoes are tender and the meat is tender and browned.

Baked Possum

Parboil a possum in salt water until it's tender. Discard the cooking water. Debone and chop the meat. Spread the meat in a baking dish that has been coated with cooking spray.

1 teaspoon celery salt
½ teaspoon garlic powder
1 teaspoon salt

Mix the spices together and sprinkle over the meat. Slice 1 large onion and separate it into rings. Spread the onion rings over the meat.

1 can beer
2 cups bottled barbecue sauce
2 tablespoons Worcestershire sauce

Mix the beer, barbecue sauce, and Worcestershire sauce together and pour over the meat and onion. Cover the baking dish tightly with foil and bake in a 325-degree oven for 2 hours or until tender. Remove the cover and let the meat brown for 30 minutes.

GROUNDHOGS OR WOODCHUCKS

Some of the most underutilized and excellent meat is that of ground-hogs or woodchucks. Chucks are actually marmots, and are called a variety of names depending on the region. The eastern or midwestern names include woodchuck, pasture pup, and groundhog. Western species include yellow-footed, yellow-bellied, rock chuck, and mountain marmot. In the Northwest you'll find mountain marmot, rock chuck, and hoary marmot. Chucks, regardless of their name or region, are considered "varmints" both by hunters and farmers and ranchers. Chucks create large burrows in fields and fencerows as well as in and around farm and ranch buildings. These burrows can damage croplands and even injure livestock. Chucks are also voracious eaters of such crops as clovers and alfalfa—they can eat as much as a third of their weight in these valuable crops a day. On the other hand, the succulent diet of chucks in many parts of the country provides a small game critter with great "taste." Many farmers and ranchers welcome hunters who'd like to go after these "varmints." In many parts of the country the most popular method of hunting is with long-range varmint rifles fitted with high-power scopes.

Groundhog is also a semidark meat, but sweet and fine textured. As with any game meat, the animal must be properly cared for in the field, dressed as soon as possible, and the meat kept cool. Chucks can range from just a half-dozen pounds to almost 20 pounds, depending on locale and species. Some of the species in the mountain states can carry Rocky Mountain spotted fever, obtained from ticks. Make sure you wear gloves when dressing groundhogs.

A groundhog should be skinned and drawn then soaked for several hours or overnight in salt water. All excess fat should be removed. Parboil, discarding the cooking water, to remove remaining fat.

Baked Groundhog

Cut a groundhog into serving-sized pieces. Parboil as described above. Salt and pepper each piece and roll it in flour. Brown in a cast-iron Dutch oven in ¼ inch of oil. When the meat is brown on both sides, cover it with boiling water, tightly cover the pan, and place it in a 350-degree oven for 1 hour or until tender.

Sweet Pepper Baked Hog

Cut a groundhog into quarters and parboil. Make sure the fat is parboiled off the groundhog. Discard the cooking liquid and debone the meat. Chop the meat into bite-sized pieces, and spread these in a large roasting pan that has been coated with cooking spray.

Salt and pepper
1 large onion, diced
1 sweet yellow pepper, diced
1 sweet green pepper, diced
3 stalks celery, diced
2 small zucchini, diced
1 teaspoon garlic powder or fresh minced garlic
1 teaspoon Italian seasoning
2 14½-ounce cans diced tomatoes with green chilies, mild or hot

Add all of the above ingredients to the meat, cover tightly, and bake at 325 degrees for 2 hours or until tender. Check after the first hour and add water or tomato juice if needed. Serve with pasta, garlic bread, and salad.

BEAVER

More famous for their fur than their meat, beavers are rare small game meat for most of us. The animals are rarely hunted; in fact, it may be illegal to hunt beavers in some states. In other areas beavers may be quite abundant, with quite liberal seasons. Regardless, beavers are usually trapped, primarily for the hide, with the amount of trapping dictated by fur prices. When their numbers aren't kept in check, beavers can be a nuisance. They can dam up small streams, and their voracious appetite for succulent bark can make short work of valuable stream or lakeside trees.

Beavers are husky animals ranging about 20 pounds for a kit (young of the year) to well over 80 pounds for a mature adult in its prime. The meat of beavers is dark red and fine textured. In young animals the meat is extremely tender and tasty. Like most small game, however, older animals can be tough. Beaver meat doesn't have the dryness of some other small game meats. Beaver-tail soup is an old trappers' survival food. A beaver tail is mostly gristle and fat with little meat value, although the old-timers probably did eat it when in dire straits.

Dressing a beaver takes work, even after the animal is skinned. It's extremely important to remove all fat and all glands, including the castor or musk glands. These two glands lie just in front of the genitals of both sexes. The glands are easily noticed, but it's important to carefully peel them away from the muscle back toward the vent before cutting them off. Above all, don't cut into them by mistake.

Beaver Stew

This recipe is another specialty of trapper Tad Brown.

1 beaver, cut into pieces
2 ribs celery
2 medium onions, quartered
1 can sliced mushrooms
2 carrots, diced
4 potatoes, cubed
1 package brown gravy mix
Salt, pepper, and flour

Parboil the beaver with the celery and 1 of the onions until tender. Remove the fat and bone, discarding the vegetables and broth. In a slow cooker, place the beaver meat, the remaining onion, and the mushrooms, carrots, and potatoes. Mix the brown gravy according to the package directions and add this, too. Add enough water to cover, along with salt and pepper. Cook over medium heat for 8 hours. Thicken with flour and water.

Tad Brown's Barbecue Beaver

1 beaver, cut into pieces
2 ribs celery
1 medium onion
1 medium apple
Barbecue sauce
Salt
1 teaspoon Liquid Smoke
½ teaspoon dry mustard
2 tablespoons brown sugar

Parboil the beaver with the celery, onion, and apple until tender. Remove the fat and bones, discarding the apple, vegetables, and broth. Place the meat in a greased casserole, cover with barbecue sauce, and stir in the remaining ingredients. Cover and bake at 300 degrees for 2 hours.

MUSKRAT

Marsh rabbit is another term for this water-loving small game animal. The name comes from the sweet taste of the meat and the fact that the animal made it into the stew pot frequently during tough times not too many years ago. In fact, "marsh rabbit" was a staple in many restaurants around the turn of the 20th century and is still a favored small game animal in states where it flourishes. Unfortunately, many folks have a tough time getting around the *rat* in the name. Although muskrats are sometimes taken by plinking hunters, for the most part they're trapped for their fur these days, with the meat an incidental by-product. Weighing from 2 to 4 pounds, this little critter is one of the "cleanest" of game animals—feeding only on vegetation and living in water for most of its life. Muskrat meat is tender but somewhat dark, and tastes a little like duck. Muskrat meat will work in just about any recipe that calls for squirrel or rabbit—or chicken, for that matter.

Again, soak the meat overnight in salt water. Make sure all fat and scent glands are removed when dressing.

Pan-Fried Muskrat with Gravy

After soaking a muskrat overnight in salt water, drain it, pat it dry, and cut it into serving-sized pieces. Lightly whip 1 egg with 1/4 cup of milk. Dip the muskrat into the egg/milk mixture, add salt and pepper, then roll it in flour. Pan fry in a large cast-iron skillet in 1/2 inch of oil over medium high until all the pieces are browned on both sides. Then lower the temperature and fry until the meat is tender. Remove the meat to a warm platter and make milk gravy in the skillet.

Marsh Rabbit Patties

1 Marsh Rabbit
Salt
1 teaspoon peppercorns
2 Stalks celery
1 Onion
1 Carrot

Carefully clean a muskrat, remove all fat and scent glands. Soak overnight in salt water. Cut the muskrat into pieces and place in a stock pot along with the celery, carrot, and onion. Cover with salted water and add the peppercorns. Simmer until the meat falls from the bones. Remove the meat from the bones.

2 cups cracker or bread crumbs
¼ cup diced onion
2 Eggs
1 teaspoon lemon juice, wine or wine vinegar

Prepare cracker or bread crumbs in a food processor. Chop the muskrat meat and onion in a food processor. Stir together the crumbs, meat, lemon juice, and slightly beaten eggs. Add a drop of milk if too dry to make into patties and salt and pepper if needed. Shape into patties and brown in hot oil, turning once. These patties are great served with creamed peas and potatoes.

Sources

Allied Kenco Sales, 800-356-5189, www.alliedkenco.com
Bass Pro Shops, 800-BASS PRO, www.basspro.com
Bill Harper's Seasonings and cookbooks, 573-346-1779
Bradley Smoker, 800-665-4188, www.bradleysmoker.com
The Brinkmann Corp., 800-527-0717, www.thebrinkmanncorp.com
Cabela's, 800-237-444, www.cabelas.com
Chef'sChoice, EdgeCraft Corp., 800-342-3255, www.edgecraft.com
Excalibur Dehydrators, www.excaliburdehydrator.com
FoodSaver, Tilia, 800-777-5452, www.foodsaver.com
Game Locker, 888-246-4342, www.gamelockercoolers.com
Good-One Smokers, Ron Goodwin Enterprises, 620-726-5281,
www.thegood-one.com
Lawry's Foods, 800-9LAWRYS, www.lawrys.com
L.E.M. Products, Inc., 877-536-7763, www.lemproducts.com
Little Chief Smoker Products, Luhr-Jensen & Sons, Inc., 800-366-
3811, www.luhrjensen.com
Masterbuilt Mfg., Inc., 800-489-1581, www.masterbuilt.com
Outland Sports, Inc., 417-451-4438, www.outlandsports.com
The Sausage Maker, Inc., 888-490-8525, www.sausagemaker.com
Weston Supply, 800-814-4895, www.westonsupply.com

Index

pressure canning, 9, 79–80

Q
Quesadillas (recipe), 109

R
Rabbit Alfredo (recipe),
   107–8
Rabbit Casserole (recipe),
   105
Rabbit Chunks (recipe), 103
Rabbit Fajitas (recipe), 107
Rabbit Fricassee (recipe),
   100–101
Rabbit Stew (recipe), 103–4,
   108–9
rabbits, ix, 11–12, *12*
   field dressing, 12–14, *13*
   recipes, 100–110
   skinning, 14, *15–18*, 18,
      19, *20*, 20–21
   tularemia danger, 21–22
rabies, 116
raccoons, vii, ix, 41, 44
   pelts of, 62
   recipes, 115–18
refrigerators, 7, 87
rock woodchuck, 120
Ron Goodwin Enterprises,
   95

S
safety precautions, *4*, 5,
   21–22, 83–84, 88, 99,
   121
Salmonella, 83

sausages, 9, 88–89, *89–93*,
   93, *94*, 95
scent glands, *55*, 74, 79, 124
sharpening devices, *3*, 3–4
shot-damaged meat, 39, 74,
   99
skinning
   beavers, 62, *62–67*, 68
   furred small game, *43*,
      43–44
      cased-skin method, 44,
         45–61, 47, 62
      open-pelt method, 62,
         62–67, 68
   muskrats, *57–61*
   rabbits, 4, 14, *15–18*, 18,
      19, *20*, 20–21
   squirrels, 4, 29–31, *30–38*
Smoked Summer Sausage
   (recipe), 88–89, *89–93*,
   93, *94*, 95
smoking, 81
   cold smoking, 87–88
   jerky, 81, *82*, 83–84,
      85–86, 86–87
   smoke cooking and
      flavoring, 95–96,
      96–98, 98
   summer sausage, 88–89,
      89–93, 93, *94*, 95
Smothered Rabbit (recipe),
   101–2
soaking, 39, 74, 88, 116, 119,
   124
South-of-the-Border Rabbit
   (recipe), 105
spoilage, 75, 84
Squirrel Stew (recipe), 113
Squirrel Under Sauerkraut
   (recipe), 114–15
squirrels, vii, ix, *23*, 23–24
   aging, 39